THE CHURCH REMEMBERS

The Historical Series of the Reformed Church in America
no. 101

THE CHURCH REMEMBERS
Papers of the RCA Commission on History,
1977 to 2019

James Hart Brumm, ed.

Reformed Church Press
Grand Rapids, Michigan

© 2020 Reformed Church Press
All rights reserved

Printed in the United States of America

ISBN: 978-1-950572-11-3

Library of Congress Control Number: 2020947195

The Historical Series of the Reformed Church in America

The series was inaugurated in 1968 by the General Synod of the Reformed Church in America acting through the Commission on History to communicate the church's heritage and collective memory and to reflect on our identity and mission, encouraging historical scholarship which informs both church and academy.

www.rca.org/series

General Editor
    James Hart Brumm, MDiv, MPhil
    New Brunswick Theological Seminary

Associate Editor
    Jeffrey Chu, MDiv
    Grand Rapids, MI

Copy Editor
    Joshua Parks
    Grand Rapids, MI

Production Editor
    Russell L. Gasero
    Archives, Reformed Church in America

Cover Design
    Matthew Gasero
    Archives, Reformed Church in America

General Editor Emeritus
    Donald J. Bruggink, PhD, DD
    Van Raalte Institute, Hope College

Commission on History
    Alexander Arthurs, Western Theological Seminary
    Lynn Japinga, PhD, Hope College
    Andrew Klumpp, MDiv, Southern Methodist University
    Steven Pierce, DMin, Grand Rapids, MI
    David M. Tripold, PhD, Monmouth University
    David Zomer, MDiv, Kalamazoo, MI

Contents

Preface: An Argument for Memory

Section 1: The Constitution

1. A Historical Understanding of Doctrinal Standards as Part of the Constitution of the Reformed Church in America (2005) — 3
2. Extra-Canonical Tests for Church Membership and Ministry (2007) — 15
3. The Evolving Understanding of Office in the Reformed Church in America: A Brief Survey (2015) — 21
4. A Look at the History of the Term "Bounds," Particularly Pertaining to Classes (2019) — 33

Section 2: The General Synod

5. To Collect and Preserve (1977) — 43
6. Historical Development of the President's Report (2004) — 49
7. An Examination of Historical Precedent for Setting RCA Policy (2007) — 55
8. History of Funding for General Synod (2019) — 63

Section 3: Being Church

9. A Historical Examination of the Relationship Among RCA Assemblies As Conceived in the Articles of Dort (1619) and the Explanatory Articles (1792) (2007) — 77
10. Commissioned Pastors in the Reformed Church in America: A Historical and Contextual Survey (2015) — 81
11. A Brief History of Schism and Separation in the Reformed Church in America Along with a Summary of the Creeds and Confessions as Statements of Unity (2016) — 95

12.	Ministerial Supply, 1900–2010: A Historical Perspective (2017)	115
13.	"Historic and Faithful Witnesses": Reflecting on the Standards and How They Have Been Used in the Forms of Declaration and the Church (2018)	133

Section 4: Church and World

14	A Historical Summary of the Actions of the General Synod with Regard to Homosexuality: 1974-2012 (2013)	143
15.	What Was the Reformation? (2016)	153
16.	Ecumenism in the RCA (2018)	157
17.	Anabaptist and Reformed Relations: A Historical Overview (2019)	167

Preface

An Argument for Memory

What is a witness if not someone who has a tale to tell and lives only with one haunting desire: to tell it. Without memory, there is no culture. Without memory, there would be no civilization, no society, no future.

After all, God is God because he remembers.[1]

Author and Holocaust survivor Elie Wiesel spoke late in his life about the importance not only of remembering things that have happened, but of telling others about them—the work of historians. And what is very nice for historians, including all of those who have done the work of the Commission on History since its inception in 1966 and the History and Research Committee that came before it, is that Wiesel points out how all of this work is theological: "God is God because (God) remembers."

---

[1] Elie Wiesel, "A God Who Remembers," *All Things Considered*, NPR Radio, April 7, 2008, accessed March 29, 2020, www.npr.org/2008/04/07/89357808/a-god-who-remembers.

A lot of Scripture is devoted to the idea of remembering. The word *remember* appears 286 times in the New Revised Standard Version[2] of the Bible, while the word *remembrance* shows up another 28 times. In the Hebrew Scriptures, God calls his people, again and again, to pile up stones or raise an *Ebenezer*—a "stone of help"—so that future generations would ask about the monument and be told about how God had been faithful to them up to that point and would see them safely through. These are occasions for the covenant to be renewed. In the Gospels, Jesus instructs his followers to share bread and cup, his body and blood, "in remembrance of me."[3] The Greek word for *remembrance* here is ἀνάμνησις (*anamnesis*), which literally means "re-membering": putting something from the past back together and making it live in the present. This, then, is the historian's task.

Unfortunately for historians, people often believe they don't want to listen to history. Most people don't seem to want to discuss the past. That may be out of some assumption that history tells stories of things that happened once and cannot be changed, or that historians will consider the "old" or "historic" solution to a problem to be the only acceptable one. Of course, those aren't historians, those are antiquarians.

No, I suspect that, on some level, we are all aware of the *anamnesis*; we are aware that good historical work means actually bringing the past into the present. As a rule, we aren't proud of certain parts of our pasts, and we have no desire to face them again. This may have something to do with the fact that the original instructions for the Commission on History gave it the task to simply advise the General Synod on the collection and preservation of official denominational records.[4] The denomination wanted its past cared for and preserved but largely kept out of the way so no one needed to face it. It was only in 2003 that the Commission was instructed to "offer a historical perspective, either

---

[2] *The Holy Bible*, New Revised Standard Version (New York: National Council of Churches, 1989) (hereafter *NRSV*). Unless otherwise noted, all Scripture quotations in this volume are from this translation.

[3] Luke 22:19.

[4] *Acts and Proceedings of the General Synod of the Reformed Church in America* (hereafter *MGS*) 1966 (Somerville, New Jersey: The Somerset Press, 1966), 315. The *Book of Church Order* (*BCO*), 3.1.5, section 5, assigns the Commission to "actively promote research on, interest in, and reflection on, the history and traditions of the RCA" (*Book of Church Order*, 2019 ed. [New York: Reformed Church Press, 2019]).

orally or in writing, on matters being presented to the General Synod."[5] Almost all the papers in this volume were written and presented after that instruction.

Since 2003, when the Commission on History was authorized to be more proactive, the General Synod began to receive its re-memberings first reluctantly and then more eagerly. Upon reading actual history, competently done, the Synod has begun to appreciate that there is always a present-day application. Following the not-so-old adage that "History never repeats itself, but it rhymes,"[6] we can all learn that, even when the past doesn't suggest possible solutions to present problems, it does help explain how we got to where we are. That, therefore, is the primary goal of the papers presented by the Commission: not to tell the Synod how it should move forward, but to remind the delegates how we have gotten to where we are, so that everyone may deliberate and discern from the same understanding.

God remembers, and when God—whose life, as C. S. Lewis suggests, "does not consist of moments following one another"[7]—re-members the past, bringing it into the present communion of the living Church and showing us our place in it, the Church needs to pay attention. Indeed, since the Church is the body of Christ, doing the work of God, we are called to do the re-membering, never abandoning what was or what will be. And yet, the Church is also fully human, like our Savior, and so we cannot embrace *all* that was and *all* that will be in the same way. Historians—and the Commission on History in particular—help us with our *anamnesis* so that we can be truly open to our future.

Because of our limited humanity, we are incapable of perceiving and processing everything at once; omniscience belongs only to God. Thus, part of the historian's task is to sort history into digestible bits, to categorize them in ways that our minds can process, understand, and

---

[5] *MGS* 2003, 159. This was not the Commission's request, nor did it come from denominational leadership, but was the result of a motion from the floor.

[6] Attributed to Mark Twain, this aphorism first appeared in print in John Robert Colombo's poem "A Said Poem" in 1970 (John Robert Colombo, *Neo Poems* [Vancouver, BC: Sono Nis Press, 1970], 46).

[7] C. S. Lewis, *Mere Christianity* (New York: Macmillan, 1952), 146. Lewis goes on to insist that "If you picture Time as a straight line along which we have to travel, then you must picture God as the whole page on which the line is drawn. We come to the parts of the line one by one: we have to leave A behind in order to get to B, and cannot reach C until we leave B behind. God, from above or outside or all around, contains the whole line, and sees it all" (147). Lewis then goes on to suggest that "God has no history" (148). I am hopeful that God still has a soft spot for the work of historians.

discuss. I repeatedly tell my own students that point of view is critical: some facts have to be more important than others so that a historian can form a coherent narrative and finish the story. This means that history always gets re-examined and re-evaluated. It also means that historians have a strong drive to sort and categorize stories and facts. In real life, most people do not constantly consider how whatever present action they might take fits into some historic trend. Historians, on the other hand, are trained to think in just that way, all the while fully aware that life is messy and doesn't fit into neat categories.

Still, this historian, seeking to make the material assigned to him more easily consumed by you, the reader, has sorted the seventeen papers presented here into four categories: *the Constitution*, or papers dealing primarily with issues that address the core of who the Reformed Church in America claims to be; *the General Synod*, or issues that primarily affect how the broadest assembly of the church functions; *Being Church*, five papers that primarily examine issues of how various assemblies, congregations, and members deal with one another; and *Church and World*, a set of papers that address how the RCA has dealt with other church bodies and issues that originated outside of the denomination itself. Astute readers will identify all sorts of ways in which these categories are entirely artificial, in which the papers here cross the lines I have created and could easily be sorted in other ways. Arguably, all of the papers could fit into one classification, or each could be a class unto itself. Neither of those are really helpful to you, the reader, however. It is my hope that this arrangement might be.

Commission papers in the Reformed Church in America are considered to be the work of the commissions that presented them. These papers have been produced by people who have been members of or consultants to the Commission on History over the past 54 years, as well as a few outside authors who have graciously accepted invitations. Since the title of this book is *The Church Remembers*, it seems appropriate to remember those people here:

Benjamin Alicea-Luogo
John Arnone
Alexander Arthurs
Bernita Babb
John W. Beardslee III**
Kenneth Bradsell*
Arie Brouwer*
George Brown Jr.***

Donald J. Bruggink***
Elton J. Bruins
James Hart Brumm***
Bette Brunsting
Douglas Carlson
Mrs. Robert Cecil**
John Coakley
Gerald F. De Jong

Kenneth Eberline
Douglas Estella
Glenna Foster
Linda Walvoord de Velder
Marion de Velder*
Roy Englehardt**
Russell L. Gasero**
Howard G. Hageman
Herman Harmelink III
Lynn Japinga
Mary Kansfield
Norman J. Kansfield
LeeAnna Keith
Nella Kennedy
E. William Kennedy
Andrew Klumpp***
Hartmut Kramer-Mills
Joseph Loux
Barbara Mahannah**
Scott Manetsch
Sophie Mathonnet-VanderWell
Melody Meeter
Christopher Moore
Deborah Morris*
Edwin Mulder*
James Z. Nettinga
John Oquendo
Monica Schaap Pierce
Steven Pierce
Jennifer Reece
Sharon Scholten
Jesus Serrano
Leroy Seuss
Elsie Stryker**
Larry J. Suntken
Robert Terwilliger
Sarah Tinkelman
David Tripold
J. Jeffrey Tyler
Douglas Van Aartsen
Peter N. VandenBerge**
James W. Van Hoeven
Matthew J. van Maastricht***
Audrea Vermilyea
Dennis Voskuil
Barbara Walvoord
Lori Witt
David Zomer[8]

There are so many other things which the church will need to remember, things we have yet to imagine. This book exists to remind readers that some of these studies have already been written. I look

---

[8] Names, listed alphabetically, come from the reports of, variously, the Commission on History, the Commission on Nominations, or the Committee on Resolutions in the *Acts and Proceedings of the General Synod* for the years 1966 through 2019. Those with a single asterisk (*) are people who served as staff to the Commission: Marion de Velder, Arie Brouwer, and Edwin Mulder all served as *ex officio* members of the Commission, while they were General Secretary. After that practice ended, Kenneth Bradsell, Deborah Morris, and Russell Gasero each staffed the Commission in turn. Those with two asterisks (**) worked for the Commission maintaining the Archives, and came primarily from the staff of Gardner A. Sage Library at New Brunswick Theological Seminary: Peter VandenBerge, then John W. Beardslee III, then, from 1978 to 2019, Russell L. Gasero, were Archivists of the RCA. Those with three asterisks (***) were staff of the Historical Series of the Reformed Church in America at one point or another, as was Gasero; all but George Brown Jr., were, at some point, also members of the Commission.

forward to a second edition of *The Church Remembers*, sometime around the year 2040, as the Commission on History continues to assemble people with passion and expertise to keep the Synod and the church informed at a very low cost—just as all the General Synod commissions do. I hope that some of you who read these papers will come up with questions of your own, dig around until you get answers, and use those answers to help office bearers and church members understand why we do what we do. That is the first step in understanding what we might be called to do next, and that, of course, is why we have memory. That is the work of historians in serving the God who remembers.

Soli Deo gloria!
James Hart Brumm
The first week of Easter, 2020

SECTION 1: THE CONSTITUTION

CHAPTER 1

A Historical Understanding of Doctrinal Standards as Part of the Constitution of the Reformed Church in America[1]

It is important to remember that the Reformation in the Netherlands, which began considerably earlier than the Dutch War of Independence from Spain, was a process of evolution as much as revolution. Luther nailed his Ninety-Five Theses to the church door in Wittenberg in 1517. By the year 1520, there was a public burning of Martin Luther's books in Louvain.[2] According to Alastair Duke, at least thirty works of Luther had appeared in Dutch translations by that same year.[3] The Great Synod of Dort, which saw the adoption of the final doctrinal standard and key elements of what we know as Reformed Church order, was a century later.

The reason the Reformation took so long to complete in the Netherlands was that the Reformation in the Netherlands went through

---

[1] *Minutes of General Synod* (hereafter *MGS*) 2005 (New York; Reformed Church Press, 2005), 148–56.
[2] Alastair Duke, *Reformation and Revolt in the Low Countries* (London: The Hambledon Press, 1990), 31.
[3] Duke, *Reformation and Revolt*, 31. Duke cites as his source C. Ch. G. Visser, *Luther's Geschriften in de Nederlanden tot 1546* (Assen, Germany: 1946), 130–33.

several stages, and, in each of these stages, was strongly resisted by the authorities of the State. The rulers of the Netherlands did all that they could to hinder, persecute, and exterminate Protestants in the Netherlands, and kept this up for many years. For most of the years of the Great Reformation, the Protestant movement and the struggling Reformed Church in the Netherlands was like a besieged city. As the Reformed believers of that day expressed themselves, for a long time they were "The Reformed Church under the Cross."

Likewise, the three Reformed confessions (the Belgic Confession, the Heidelberg Catechism and its Compendium, and the Canons of the Synod of Dort), along with the three ecumenical creeds, were adopted as doctrinal standards through a process of evolution, which began before there was such an idea as "standards." The term "standards" developed after the fact as a term to describe their commonality. In the sixteenth and seventeenth centuries, the period of Dutch Reformed formation, the church had not yet determined that it needed something called standards, and then decided which ones they should choose. The fact that we call them "standards," emphasizing their commonality, actually bears witness to our relative distance from them and from their original function.

The Belgic Confession

The Belgic Confession was adopted along the model of earlier confessions—the Augsburg and the First Helvetic. The Protestant confession as a genre had already evolved sufficiently for the form to be recognized as functional and necessary. Thus, when Guido de Bres wrote his confession, it was not just for the King of Spain, but also for the churches with which he was associated. The new Protestant congregations found themselves in a revolutionary situation, and needed something to provide stability—a standard of unity, as it would come to be called.

The Belgic Confession was first accepted by a Walloon (French-speaking) regional synod in the southern Netherlands. Leyden University professor L. Knappertt says that a synod held at Armentiers (circa 1563) declared that ministers and elders must subscribe to the Belgic Confession.[4] But the form of that subscription is interesting, as noted in this record of an early official acceptance of the confession at a synod held at La Vigne, near Antwerp, in 1565:

---

[4] L. Knappert, *Het Ontstaan en Vestiging van het Protestantisme in de Nederlanden* (*The Origin and Establishment of Protestantism in the Low Countries*) (Utrecht: A. Oosthoek, 1924), 322.

> At the opening of each Synod the Confession of Faith of this country shall be read out in order to demonstrate our unity and to [allow] consideration whether it should be changed or amended.[5]

The Belgic Confession was adopted by the various "churches under the cross," and eventually came to be adopted by the various provincial governments, resulting in its first real constitutional status. The three creeds were adopted *ad seriatum* along with the Belgic Confession, as they are identified at the close of Belgic Article nine: "And so, in this matter we willingly accept the three ecumenical creeds—the Apostles', Nicene, and Athanasian—as well as what the ancient fathers decided in agreement with them."[6] Yet, in at least some cases, such as the La Vigne Synod, this adoption was somewhat provisional, allowing for changes in the received text, as if it was meant to be an evolving document for an evolving understanding of the church.

The Heidelberg Catechism

The Heidelberg Catechism is an example of resources adopted by the refugee churches that operated outside of the Netherlands for much of the sixteenth century. The city of Heidelberg was also where the Dutch refugee congregations saw how the neighboring Reformed churches of an area were organized into a classis, a principle which they took back home with them.[7] Peter Dathens—also known as Petrus Dathenus—translated the catechism into the Dutch language; it was written when he was in Heidelberg, and he may have contributed to its content.

The Heidelberg Catechism, however, had a purpose different from the Belgic Confession. The catechism was adopted really as a common curriculum, a teaching tool for all churches. It was not adopted as a doctrinal standard in the same way as the confession was, but as the curriculum enforced on all pastors and schoolteachers, beginning among the scattered congregations and later becoming constitutional when the provinces began to adopt and enforce it.

---

[5] "The Reformed Church Under the Cross: Extracts from the So-Called Walloon Synods, 1563-1565," Universiteit Leiden, accessed February 13, 2004, dutchrevolt. leidenuniv/Sources%20English/15631565.

[6] Belgic Confession (translation adopted in 1991), Reformed Church in America, www.rca.org/resources/belgic-confession.

[7] Bernard Vogler, *Les Inspecteurs Ecclésiastiques Protestantes en Territoire Rhénans, Revue d'Histoire et de Philosophie Religieuses*, Tome LIV (1974), 91.

Evidence suggests that, as with the Belgic Confession, adoption of the Heidelberg Catechism followed an evolutionary process. At the Synod of Emden (1571), the Dutch-speaking ministers were asked to subscribe to the French (Gallican) Confession, and the French-speaking (Walloon) ministers were asked to subscribe to the Netherlandic (Belgic) Confession to demonstrate their basic unity.[8] This is a bit strange, and demonstrates the confusion of those times, since a French-speaking (Walloon) Synod had already officially accepted the Belgic Confession in 1561. They also decided that the Heidelberg Catechism should be adopted as the official catechism, but added that churches that already used another good catechism were free to continue using it.[9]

The Canons of Dort

The Canons of Dort were first adopted as law for the Netherlands, as a great footnote to the Belgic Confession. Originally, it was proposed to rewrite the Belgic. But then it was thought better to keep the Belgic as is and prepare the huge footnote. The Canons of Dort are canons in the strict sense of the word. In Dutch they're called *Leer-regels*, measuring sticks for teaching/doctrine. The Great Synod, when adopting them, used the language of "adding them to the public documents of the church." The synod did not seem to use the precise terminology "doctrinal standards." The public documents included the confession, catechism, liturgy, and church order. This was a common set of documents which each province was free to adapt as it chose, although in colonies and crown lands, so to speak, the public documents were to be used unaltered. And then, since the States General refused to call another General Synod, no change in any of the public documents was possible to effect, since only a General Synod could do this. Over the centuries of this status quo, one can well expect that their standing sometimes changed from function to landmark to monument.

It is unclear when "doctrinal standards" as a term and collective concept began to be used. In the American colonies, the language used most often was the "Netherlandish Constitution," including all the so-called public documents. Eventually, the three doctrinal standards came to be identified as a specific group, but under the more frequently used term *Formulieren van Eenigheit*, or "Formulae of Concord." That Corwin

---

[8] Hooijer, *Oude Kerkenordeningen*, 67.
[9] Hooijer, *Oude Kerkenordeningen*, 67.

translates this phrase as "Formulas of Unity"[10] says a lot about how the RCA as a denomination was coming to be viewed by the dawn of the twentieth century. Corwin also seems to link the term "Standards" to the fact that all ministers of Word and sacrament and professors of theology are required to subscribe to these formulae, and have been since 1619. Colonial Reformed ministers, however, were also required to subscribe to the "Fundamental Articles" of the Coetus from 1738 to 1771 (Conferentie ministers also subscribed to these, but signed a separate book), and to the "Articles of Union" from 1771 to 1792,[11] but these do not seem to have attained the same status as the doctrinal standards.

The Standards were already constitutional long before the Explanatory Articles by virtue of their having been part of the general constitution of the Dutch republic; they were established by law in each province. The Duke's Laws, which allowed for the survival of the Dutch church in the British colonies after New Netherland fell to the English, were understood as requiring the Dutch congregations to adhere to the established Dutch church. The U.S. War for Independence changed all that. The 1793 Constitution was simply an attempt to adapt an Erastian constitution for a free-church setting. It certainly doesn't seem that, by the end of the eighteenth century, anybody remembered the fluid attitude toward the Heidelberg Catechism and the Belgic Confession present at their inception. And since, according to Daniel Meeter,[12] one of the chief purposes of the 1793 Constitution was to find things to be conservative about in a time of revolution, one can hardly expect any thought to be countenanced on providing a rule that allows for changing the doctrinal standards in any way.

Indeed, Meeter points out that by making the Standards constitutional, the church could not change its confessions "without changing itself."[13] No historic Calvinist church, after the time of Westminster, would have found it conceivable to even consider revising or adding to its doctrinal standards. And so it was in the Reformed Church in America until 1959, when an overture from the Classis of

---

[10] Edward Tanjore Corwin, *A Digest of Constitutional and Synodical Legislation of the Reformed Church in America* (New York: Board of Publication of the Reformed Church in America, 1906), 688.

[11] Corwin, *Digest*, 709.

[12] Daniel J. Meeter, *Meeting Each Other in Doctrine, Liturgy, and Government*, The Historical Series of the Reformed Church in America 24 (Grand Rapids, MI: Eerdmans, 1993), 39, 45.

[13] Meeter, *Meeting Each Other*, 39.

Pella called for a new confession of faith "that will give expression to our Christian faith on the basis of Scripture, the historic creeds, and the Reformed Standards of Unity, in the light of present day needs and experiences."[14] This led to the formation of the Commission on Theology.[15] The commission was expected both to revise the Doctrinal Standards to make them more relevant and/or compatible with the contemporary scene, and to produce a new confession of faith.

With reference to the revision of the Standards, discussions in the new commission started with such an obvious item as the statement that "Mass is fundamentally a complete denial of the once for all sacrifice and passion of Jesus Christ and as such an idolatry to be condemned." That was followed by another easy issue, i.e., that we "hate the Anabaptists." After that, however, things got a bit sticky. Many members of the commission had their own pet complaints about the Standards. It soon became evident that except for the above, there was marked disagreement on every issue raised. At that point the discussion returned to where it should have begun, that is, that the Standards are historic documents and are to be understood within the context of their time. As such, they are to remain as written, and while commentary on them is appropriate, changing them is not.[16]

Study of an Experiment: Our Song of Hope

What follows are the first-person recollections of Eugene Heideman, who was appointed by the RCA General Synod in 1970 to serve as secretary of a committee to prepare a new confessional statement to be submitted to the RCA for consideration and approval. He was appointed and became the author of the statement that came to bear the title Our Song of Hope (after more than a decade of discussion about the need for a new confessional statement).

> It is possible that the impetus for the Pella overture (see above) came from Gerrit Vander Lugt. I had been studying in the Netherlands, 1954-56, and had written one or more articles in the Reformed Review about the role of confessional statements in the RCA. Dr. Vander Lugt in about 1957 told me of his great interest in the confessional statement *Fundementen en Perspectieven*,

---

[14] *MGS* 1959, 123.
[15] James I. Cook, ed., *The Church Speaks: Papers of the Commission on Theology*, The Historical Series of the Reformed Church in America 15 (Grand Rapids, MI: Eerdmans, 1985), 11.
[16] This summarizes material which can be found in Cook, *The Church Speaks*, 11-28.

prepared for the Nederlandse Hervormde Kerk (NHK), and said it may be time for the RCA to carry on such a project. There were others in the RCA who were paying careful attention to events in the NHK, so it is possible that Vander Lugt was just one of a number of persons interested in such a project. The overture reached the floor of the General Synod through the Commission on Unity, so there was an ecumenical aspect to the project from the very beginning.

The Commission on Theology (CT) presented "A Confession of Faith" to the General Synod of 1966 with the recommendation that it be sent to the classes for study and response. In 1968, the CT reported to the General Synod that it was grateful for the responses received, but believed it to be unwise "to go any further with the present document." It believed that there was an inherent confusion in its mandate. On the one hand, it called for a rewriting of the older confessional statements in more contemporary form, but not to go beyond them, and, on the other hand, it asked that items be introduced which were not in the older creeds. This inherent confusion had "contributed to the unimpressive character of the Confession" that had been presented. The CT concluded that it was hopeless to modify the proposed statement adequately to have it accepted. It did recommend that the document be used in churches as a teaching document. To the best of my knowledge, few if any churches followed that recommendation.

The CT further commented that the church was not in the mood to give serious thought to a new statement of faith. Some were scandalized to think that the commission "had the effrontery to even think of writing a new creed." But thousands of others "could not care less" about a new confessional statement.

Nevertheless, the CT unanimously felt "constrained" to direct the thought of the church to the great need for a new and creative venture in creed-making, following the example of the United Presbyterian Church's confession of 1967 on reconciliation. It also proposed that the General Synod appoint an ad hoc committee to prepare a new statement, with only one assignment. It proposed that the new confession should stand in the tradition of the old statements, but not be a revision of them. It should have a cutting edge for the cultural climate of the day.

In 1969, the CT called again for work on a new confession, expressing the "desire for a brief statement to be used with church membership classes, to say nothing of the need for a concise statement of the faith of the Reformed Church in America that would witness to the present generation. Such a statement should be well-ordered, organized around a central theme."

In 1970, following our return from missionary service in India, Dr. Lester Kuyper, president of the General Synod, asked me to accept the assignment as secretary of the ad hoc committee. My first response to Dr. Vander Lugt's thought more than a decade before had been that I felt that the RCA should first give more attention to the statements it already had before attempting to write a new statement. In 1970 I was still ambivalent about the project. However, I wrote back to Dr. Kuyper that I was ready to try to develop such a statement if a whole series of committee meetings with constant revisions in drafts could be avoided. I proposed an alternative approach by which the whole denomination could be invited to be involved from the very beginning.

1. Before any writing would begin, a letter would be sent to every church in the denomination asking for Sunday bulletins and any other statements they had developed for their own use.
2. That the statement would be so written that it could function well in Sunday morning worship as well as in teaching new members about the faith of the RCA. On the basis of the affirmation made by Otto Noordmans and A. A. van Ruler in the Netherlands that a creed was not only a staff on which to lean for the church's journey, but also a song to be sung along the way, I hoped that the confessional would also be singable.
3. That a small amount of money be allocated for printing and postal costs and for travel for me to consult with the theological commission, RCA seminary faculty and students, and classes and congregations.

Dr. Kuyper wrote back that the General Synod accepted my suggestions, and I was appointed.

The first year was spent sending the letter to every congregation and to a selected number of RCA members who knew the denomination well, reading pertinent articles in several decades of the *Church Herald*, going through minutes of General Synod, and studying the Liturgy in order to become familiar with the history of the Standards in the RCA. That year also included reading confessional statements prepared in other denominations, including Asian denominations, talking with RCA members, and especially informal listening to students in Central College, where I was teaching, with the purpose of hearing what their generation was thinking about. The responses from congregations were collated according to subject matter.

In the summer of 1971, I spent one week reviewing all that had been accumulated and collated, reread the three Standards of Unity, and then sat at our kitchen table for five mornings and wrote the first draft that included a refrain at the beginning, twenty-four stanzas, and a prayer at the end. Two or three groups of eight people then spent one or more evenings reading the draft aloud to test for suitability for unison reading in worship. Afterwards it was sent to about fifty people in the RCA for comment.

During 1972 and 1973, the newly revised 1971 draft was made available to anyone who asked for it. I traveled to a number of areas of the RCA, met with seminary personnel, met with several classes, and corresponded with whoever wanted to correspond. At one of the meetings, the Rev. James Baar had suggested a title for the draft, "A Song of Hope," which eventually was changed to *Our Song of Hope*.

Our Song of Hope was presented to the General Synod in 1974 together with a report I had written.[17] In order that it could be received in the context of worship, morning worship services were ordered around the document, and the refrain and prayer at the end were sung. The music for the refrain and prayer was prepared at the last minute by the Rev. Don Jansma and Dr. Davis Folkerts at Central College. The music was included in the study book, which was printed to assist the RCA in its use and study of the statement between 1974 and 1978. Unfortunately, several errors crept into the notation in the study book, which made it difficult to use. Several other people set the refrain and prayer to music. The most successful of these was composed by Roger Reitberg, organist at Third Reformed Church in Holland, Michigan.

Because of my own understanding of how confessional statements need time to live in the church before they become

---

[17] See *MGS* 1974, 165-69.

part of its legal structure, I had wanted to allow for a ten-year process for use before it would be sent to the classes for adoption (1984 seemed like a good year to confess again that this world belongs to God, in contrast to a lot of popular interest in George Orwell's *1984*). However, General Synod officers and staff as well as other members of the General Synod Executive Committee believed that would be too long a period, and suggested a four-year period, to end in 1978.

Our Song of Hope was well received at the 1974 synod, and it was designated as a "provisional standard" for a period of four years, ending in 1978. This meant that the synod expected that it would be widely used; in the event that the RCA issued an edition of the Standards of Unity, it would be included as an appendix; and at the end of the four-year period or earlier, the church would decide whether to grant full status by means of a constitutional amendment.

It is difficult to know how widely *Our Song of Hope* was used during the four-year period. Where it was used, it was usually appreciated. However, the process also confirmed the conclusion of the CT of 1968 that in the RCA there are thousands who have little interest in studying the older confessions and even more perhaps "who could not care less" about adding another one.

In 1978 I submitted a report to the General Synod which recommended that "the General Synod approve Our Song of Hope as a statement of the church's faith for use in its ministry of witness, teaching, and worship."[18] My sense is that this action of the General Synod has stood the test of time. Where the statement is known and used, it continues to be profitable and challenging. From time to time I meet people who are members of congregations that use it, and they speak appreciatively about it, so it remains a valued part of my personal history. A study by Luidens and Nemeth about fifteen years ago indicated that it was known by a minority of RCA members.

Our Song of Hope has received a certain amount of interest from other denominations. It has also been included with other twentieth-century Reformed confessional statements in a book produced about a decade ago by the World Alliance of Reformed Churches.

---

[18] *MGS* 1978, 36-37. This action was approved, and Our Song of Hope continues to hold this status, but it is not a doctrinal standard of the RCA.

Conclusions

The 1968 remarks of the Commission on Theology need to be taken seriously: the church needs to pay more attention to its existing Standards before adopting new ones. It is important to notice the evolutionary process by which the creeds and most of the confessions became Standards. Decades, in the case of the Heidelberg Catechism and the Belgic Confession, and centuries, in the case of the creeds, passed before these documents achieved any sort of constitutional status. During that time, there were ample opportunities for revision and amendment, and even for experimenting with other creeds. Only the Canons of Dort gained a prompt legal standing, and it could be argued that this confession, while respected, is not beloved and quoted throughout the RCA in the same way as the other two.

Then there is Meeter's observation that when we change the Standards in the Constitution, we change the nature of the Reformed Church in America. The Explanatory Articles codified a sort of calcification that had taken place in the life of the church. The texts of our Standards became frozen in time; even updates to the translations are now part of the legitimately cumbersome amendment process. The modern Form of Declaration for Ministers, with its identification of the Standards as "historic and faithful witnesses," further solidifies that status, because it is irresponsible to try to change history.

History, however, did not stop in 1793. We are a church that is called to be reformed and ever reforming according to the Word of God. Prior to the Great Synod of Dort, doctrinal statements—"formulae of concord"—were treated as part of that continuing reformation. They also reflected one of the great strengths of Reformed polity, bubbling up from local situations into the attention of more general synods. In the American context, the Standards are imposed from above, although local congregations and assemblies are protected by the fact that there never has been a provision for changing or adding to these doctrinal statements. This may well reflect the nature of the RCA, unsure about whether we are a denomination as franchise, led from the top down, or a very Reformed collection of classes, driven by a concord of local situations. But common sense, if not experience, tells us that who the RCA is has continued and will continue to change: our government is fluid, with pieces constantly coming and going; our Liturgy, while never leaving the old behind, constantly adds new layers; only our doctrine is static.

This may have something to do with the relative disinterest that greeted *Our Song of Hope* and the efforts at revision of doctrinal standards that preceded it. The Standards stopped evolving while the church continued evolving, leaving local churches that have very little connection to what capable theologians sought to revise and update.

So we are left with the questions of whether we actually want to restart this sort of doctrinal evolution and, if so, just how we might best do that. There is a polity question: just what sort of a process needs to be created to add a standard? And there is a process question: how do we make a new standard not only legally accepted but internalized and loved by the church, when it doesn't rise up from local situations but originates at the General Synod level, and when local congregations have very little understanding of or appreciation for the intended function of the Standards in our ecclesiastical life? Until we can answer these questions coherently and effectively, it is difficult to envision how a new doctrinal standard can be added to our Constitution.

CHAPTER 2

Extra-Canonical Tests for Church Membership and Ministry[1]

Precedent in the Reformed Church in America is against the establishment of extra-canonical tests for individual church membership or ministerial office.

For clarification, extra-canonical is here used to describe any tests beyond those required in the Liturgy of the Reformed Church in America, and because the Liturgy is a part of the Constitution of the RCA, thus the Constitution as well. It should be noted that for church membership the requirements are stated in the broadest possible terms, the most specific of which are the acceptance "of the Scriptures of the Old and New Testaments as the only rule for faith and life?"[2] One is also asked to accept the "spiritual guidance of the Church."[3] The attached phrase found in the previous liturgy, "obeying its doctrines and

---

[1] *Minutes of General Synod* (hereafter *MGS*) 2007 (New York: Reformed Church Press, 2007), 302–06.
[2] *Worship the Lord: The Liturgy of the Reformed Church in America* (New York: Reformed Church Press, 2005), 34.
[3] *Worship the Lord: The Liturgy of the Reformed Church in America*, 35.

teachings," is omitted.[4] Similarly, for ministers of Word and sacrament, the most specific request is, "Do you believe the books of the Old and New Testaments to be the Word of God and the perfect doctrine of salvation; rejecting all contrary beliefs?"[5] In signing the "Declaration for Ministers of Word and Sacrament" the candidate also subscribes to the doctrinal standards of the church: the Belgic Confession, the Heidelberg Catechism, and the Canons of the Synod of Dort. The genius of these broad affirmations is that any perceived failure to live up to these commitments must be adjudicated on a case by case basis by the appropriate body: the consistory for church members, the classis for ministers of Word and sacrament.

The most crucial test of this principle occurred in the mid-nineteenth century in the controversy over Freemasonry, which pitted the recently arrived immigrant church in the Midwest against the older, largely Americanized RCA in the East.

Modern Freemasonry began in England circa 1717, and in 1723 the London Grand Lodge adopted a constitution written by the Rev. James Anderson. Its religious outlook was essentially Deistic, the constitution requiring members only to hold "to that religion in which all men agree, leaving their particular opinions to themselves."[6] In Europe Freemasonry was widely regarded as an anti-church secret society dedicated to the ideals of the Enlightenment. Pope Clement XII issued a bull of excommunication against Freemasons in 1738 on the basis that they "are men of all sects and religions, bound together by a natural morality; this bond is secret with an oath enforced by exaggerated penalties."[7] Among nineteenth century European immigrants to the United States, Reformed, Lutheran, Roman Catholic, and Orthodox alike were against Freemasonry.

In the United States, many of the late eighteenth century Founding Fathers had been Freemasons and church members. It is widely believed that it was the Freemasons of St. Andrews Lodge in Boston who participated in the Boston Tea Party. Paul Revere was also a Mason. Of the fourteen presidents of the United States that have been Freemasons, George Washington was the first (Gerald Ford the most recent). Nine signers of the Declaration of Independence, and

---

[4] James R. Esther and Donald J. Bruggink, eds., *Worship the Lord* (Grand Rapids, MI: Eerdmans, 1987), 20.
[5] *Worship the Lord; The Liturgy of the Reformed Church in America*, 149.
[6] *Encyclopaedia Judaica*, vol. 7 (New York: Macmillan, 1971), 122.
[7] *New Catholic Encyclopedia*, vol 3 (Detroit: Gale, 2003), 790.

thirteen of the Constitution were Masons.[8] While still a secret society, it was not anti-clerical, and its members did not find being Christians and Lodge members antithetical. Members of the RCA in the East, having experienced the euphoria of the birth of a new nation in the late eighteenth century, embraced the institutions of the Founding Fathers, including Freemasonry, as a positive component of the new nation. Thus the stage was set for conflict within the church, with two opposing views of the same institution.

Perceiving Freemasonry as anti-biblical and anti-Christian, Reformed Christians in the Midwest wished the General Synod to condemn Freemasonry and ban membership in the Order. Perceiving Freemasonry as a respectable American institution with respect for the Bible and having biblical components, many Reformed Christians in the East saw no conflict between the their very conservative, mission-minded, orthodox Reformed theology and membership in the Masonic Order.[9]

The issue of Freemasonry first appeared in the Minutes of the Classis Holland in 1853 when the classis declared that it was unlawful for a church member to belong to a Masonic Lodge.[10] This was the accepted European Reformed position and it was not thought necessary to codify the opinion of classis as an extra-canonical test[11] Freemasonry became a matter of controversy in 1867 when the fledgling Christian Reformed Church (CRC), having begun its separation in 1858, now established an extra-canonical test for membership by banning lodge membership by synodical order.[12] Since the cause of the CRC secession could be broadly described as dissatisfaction with practices of the RCA which were not in conformity with the secessionist outlook of the Netherlands, the Midwestern members of the RCA, being of the same mind on the Masonic issue, felt constrained to ask their General Synod

---

[8] *Encyclopedia Americana*, vol. 18 (Danbury, CT: Grolier, 1994), 432.

[9] Turretin was still being taught at New Brunswick even as John Henry Livingston proclaimed world mission in expectation of Christ's imminent return. See "The Everlasting Gospel," in *Vision from the Hill*, ed. John W. Beardslee, The Historical Series of the Reformed Church in America 12, 1-26 (Grand Rapids, MI: Eerdmans, 1984).

[10] Elton J. Bruins and Robert P. Swierenga, *Family Quarrels in the Dutch Reformed Churches in the 19th Century: The Pillar Church Sesquicentennial Lectures*, The Historical Series of the Reformed Church in America 32 (Grand Rapids, MI: Eerdmans, 1999), 114.

[11] *Classis Holland—Minutes A.D. 1848-1858* (Grand Rapids, MI: Eerdmans, 1943), 144.

[12] Bruins and Swierenga, *Family Quarrels*, 114.

to "discountenance" Freemasonry and "deliver a distinct utterance of its disapprobation of the connection of the Lord's people with the Order of Freemasons..." The General Synod voted to take no action by a vote of eighty-nine to nineteen.[13] It should be noted that the overture had stopped short of requesting an extra-canonical test which would bar church membership to Masons, although that was probably the intent.

In the following year, Classis Wisconsin again joined Holland in overturning General Synod "with reference to Freemasonry,"[14] "which was referred to a special committee."[15]

The committee of six, which included Philip Phelps of Holland, reported to the next synod. In the elegant language of the period, they concluded that "the path of prudence and safety lies outside of all oath bound secret societies..." and that "the Christian Church possesses, in its holy teachings, and its pledges of mutual love, a far higher capacity for the development of practical benevolence than can be found in the moral lessons of any mere human organization." However, the committee also stated "We cannot think, however, that they expect from Synod such a deliverance as would authorize Consistories to exclude Free Masons from church fellowship, *for this would be to establish a new and unauthorized test of membership in the Christian Church, and would interfere with consistorial prerogatives.*"[16]

With reference to the first point, the establishment of "a new and unauthorized test for membership," the formal, canonical requirements for church membership are found in the Liturgy's "Office for the Reception into Communicant Membership," essentially belief in the Old and New Testaments. Christians in the Midwest saw Freemasonry as anti-biblical. Many Christians in the East saw no biblical impediment to membership. To have added a test for church membership would have contradicted the biblical interpretation and conscience of other Christians.

The synod wisely refused a "new test of church membership," respecting the biblical understanding of both groups. Secondly, it is the elders of the church who are to decide on whether the profession of faith of the applicant is satisfactory. Neither the classis nor the synod are to usurp this function.[17]

---

[13] *MGS* 1868, 461, 463.
[14] *MGS* 1869, 551-52.
[15] *MGS* 1869, 622.
[16] *MGS* 1870, 96-97, emphasis added.
[17] Allan J. Janssen, *Constitutional Theology: Notes on the Book of Church Order of the Reformed Church in America*, The Historical Series of the Reformed Church in America 33 (Grand Rapids, MI: Eerdmans, 2000), 46-49, 80-83.

When all of the Midwestern classes again overtured synod in 1880, while synod's reply regarding secret societies was more severe, it did not back down on its refusal to add extracanonical tests for church membership or ministerial office. "No communicant members, and no minister of the Reformed Church in America ought to unite with or to remain in any society or institution, whether secret or open, whose principles and practices are anti-Christian, or contrary to the faith and practice of the Church to which he belongs ... That this synod also advises Consistories and Classes of the Church to be very kind and forbearing, and strictly constitutional in their dealings with individuals on this subject, and that they be and are hereby affectionately cautioned *against setting up any new or unauthorized tests of communion in the Christian Church.*"[18] And that was the last synodical word on extracanonical test for over a century.

The next major theological dispute in the nineteenth century concerned the "Mercersburg theology" of the German Reformed Church with which the RCA was considering a form of union. In brief, the conflict was over incorrectly perceived "Romanizing" tendencies in the German Reformed Church. While the result was to terminate all discussion with the German Reformed Church concerning any further cooperation, at no time did it result in even the suggestion of any extra-canonical test for membership or ministry.[19]

In the major dispute of the twentieth century, the ordination of women, the two principles enunciated in 1870 and 1880 continued to be observed. Sincere Christians in the Reformed Church were divided as to whether the biblical evidence allowed for or denied the ordination of women to the offices of the church. At no time did synod even consider this issue as requiring an extra-canonical test for church membership. Even when synod voted that the *Book of Church Order* allowed the ordination of women, it established a conscience clause that allowed those who believed the Bible to be against such ordination to be able to refrain from participating in such ordinations without being subject to any censure.[20] Despite the extreme differences of opinion, at no time were these differences seen as a reason for an extra-canonical test which

---

[18] *MGS* 1880, 536, emphasis added.
[19] Herman Harmelink III, *Ecumenism and the Reformed Church,* The Historical Series of the Reformed Church in America 1 (Grand Rapids, MI: Eerdmans, 1968), 32-35, 38-52. See Harmelink for more details on reactions in the RCA to the Mercersburg Theology as well.
[20] *MGS* 1980, 275; *Book of Church Order*, 2005 ed. (New York: Reformed Church Press, 2005), II.2.8, 30. Cf. Janssen, *Constitutional Theology*, 109.

would deny church membership, or ministerial status, to opposing ministers.

However, the synod of 2004 moved precipitously to insert an extra-canonical test into the Book of Church Order, which in turn opened the door to denying membership and ministerial status to any not conforming to this new and unauthorized test of membership. The circumstances surrounding this change in long-standing precedent took place on the floor of synod with little if any consideration of far reaching consequences. An overture was sent to synod by the Classis of Canadian Prairies asking synod "to affirm that marriage is properly defined as the union of one man and one woman, to the exclusion of all others."[21] The overture was recommended by the advisory committee.[22] From the floor of synod a motion was made to amend the motion by adding "To direct the Commission on Church Order to consider an amendment to the *Book of Church Order* which places this affirmation into our church order, for report to the 2005 General Synod."[23] The synod voted for this extracanonical test seemingly unaware of overturning a longstanding precedent.

Fortunately, its referral to the Commission on Church Order allowed a more careful consideration of the matter. Reporting to the synod of 2005, the commission noted that the prior action of the synod of 2004 did "not carry the weight of definitive church teaching. The General Synod does not have among its powers the determination of what, finally, is the 'teaching of the church.' In Reformed church order, the teaching of the church is determined by the creeds and confessions of the church."[24] In brief, the commission affirmed the traditional stand of the church against extra-canonical tests. But the Commission on Church Order also reaffirmed the polity of the church in noting that "the conduct of ministers has been and remains under the purview of the classis. Inserting a regulation that affects the conduct of the minister in one matter opens the question of what should be added to such a list. This commission deems it wiser to leave the matter to the classes."[25] The position of the synods of 1870 and 1880 was again upheld.

---

[21] *MGS* 2004, 332.

[22] The first reason given cited the "time-honored biblical mandate" which seemingly ignored, in terms of biblical literalism, such notables as Isaac, David, and Solomon, all of whom combined one man with more than one woman. The next three reasons were reflections of the political "cultural values" campaign which of late comes to the fore every two years.

[23] *MGS* 2004, 333.

[24] *MGS* 2005, 91.

[25] *MGS* 2005, 91.

CHAPTER 3

The Evolving Understanding of Office in the Reformed Church in America: A Brief Survey[1]

In a time when the Reformed Church in America (RCA) has, for more than half a century,[2] been discussing the number of offices we think might be necessary in the life of the church and the role of those offices in the life of congregations, this paper doesn't seek to delve into those issues. Nor does this paper seek to define what "office" should mean for the church going forward. Rather, at a time when so much energy is being invested by synods and classes discussing how and by whom ministry should be done, when our order constitutes ministries and assemblies through office, this paper seeks to reflect on how we have understood the term, as a basis for further study and discussion.

Various ministries are mentioned in the New Testament, and Paul makes well-known lists of them in Romans 12, 1 Corinthians

---

[1] *Minutes of General Synod* (hereafter *MGS* 2015 (New York: Reformed Church Press, 2015) 203-08.

[2] The State of Religion report to the General Synod of 1962 called on the synod "to ask the Theological Commission to study the Reformed doctrine of the ministry and to re-state its meaning in terms relevant to our times" (*MGS* 1962, 285, qtd. in James I. Cook, ed., *The Church Speaks: Papers of the Commission on Theology*, The Historical Series of the Reformed Church in America 15 [Grand Rapids, MI: Eerdmans, 1985], 112).

12, and Ephesians 4. None of these lists are identical, and it doesn't seem that they were meant to be exhaustive. What does seem to be clear from the Scriptures is an intent to organize congregations around certain governing ministries that are also seen to be gifts of the spirit: apostles, evangelists, ministers, elders/ bishops—these terms are used simultaneously and nearly interchangeably in many places in Scripture.[3] While, as Jim Brownson writes in a 2003 article published in *Reformed Review*, "the spiritual gifts given to the church and the ministry roles identified in the New Testament were more diverse than the formal offices that were created,"[4] we still find an evolving situation where, as the church moves forward, ministers, elders, and deacons are the offices to which people are ordained, perhaps because of their relationship to the proclamation of the Word.

By the time John Calvin was establishing the church in Geneva and the foundations of what would become the Reformed tradition, the role of bishop had come to mean something quite separate from that of elder, something tied to an organizational system modeled on the Roman military, something of which, as it was constituted in the sixteenth century, Calvin was quite suspicious.[5] Calvin decided that the offices of apostle, prophet, and evangelist were meant to be temporary, "only for that time during which churches were to be erected where none existed before."[6] These were to be appointed directly by Christ. "Next come pastors and teachers, whom the church can never go without," who were to "hold on to the faithful word."[7] Deacons were to concentrate on the care of the poor—while they have evangelism functions in the New Testament, the Reformers considered the world of the sixteenth century to be fully evangelized[8]—while elders were given the exercise of discipline.[9] All of these were to be ordained, as a means

---

[3] See Jim Brownson, "Elder-Pastors and Deacon-Evangelists: The Plurality of Offices and the Marks of the Church," *Reformed Review* 56, no. 3 (2003): 235-48.
[4] Brownson, "Elder-Pastors and Deacon-Evangelists," 238.
[5] In book four of his *Institutes* and the "Prefatory Address" to that work directed at King Francis, Calvin decries the corruption of the hierarchy of the Church of Rome, the personal wealth amassed by bishops, and the fact that they were not elected by the people. But it is less clear that he had trouble with the notion of bishops *per se*; indeed, Reformed churches in Hungary have bishops. See John Calvin, *Institutes of the Christian Religion*, trans. Ford Lewis Battles and ed. John T. McNeill (Philadelphia: Westminster Press, 1960), 14-18, 1063-64.
[6] Calvin, *Institutes*, IV:III:4, 1057.
[7] Calvin, *Institutes*, IV:III:7, 1059.
[8] Calvin, *Institutes*, IV:III:9, 1061.
[9] Calvin, *Institutes*, IV:III:8, 1060.

for ministers who came before to confer "the visible graces of the Spirit" upon those who were set aside to continue these crucial ministries.[10]

The sixteenth century confessions reinforced the idea that ministers, elders, and deacons, working together, bring order to the life of the church. As the Belgic Confession states:

> We believe that this true church
> ought to be governed according to the spiritual order
> that our Lord has taught us in his Word.
> There should be ministers or pastors
> to preach the Word of God
> and administer the sacraments.
> There should also be elders and deacons,
> along with the pastors,
> to make up the council of the church.
> By this means
> true religion is preserved;
> true doctrine is able to take its course;
> and evil people are corrected spiritually and held in check,
> so that also the poor
> and all the afflicted
> may be helped and comforted
> according to their need.[11]

The offices are defined by God's Word, and the choice of those who occupy those offices, while determined by an election, is ultimately guided by God (which is consistent with the Reformed idea that the Holy Spirit acts through the assembled people). This means they must also be treated as God's chosen emissaries:

> We believe that
> ministers of the Word of God, elders, and deacons
> ought to be chosen to their offices
> by a legitimate election of the church,
> with prayer in the name of the Lord,
> and in good order,
> as the Word of God teaches.
> So all must be careful
> not to push themselves forward improperly,

---

[10] Calvin, *Institutes*, IV:IV:16, 1067.
[11] Belgic Confession, article 30.

> but must wait for God's call,
> so that they may be assured of their calling
> and be certain that they are chosen by the Lord.
> As for the ministers of the Word,
> they all have the same power and authority,
> no matter where they may be,
> since they are all servants of Jesus Christ,
> the only universal bishop,
> and the only head of the church.

Moreover, to keep God's holy order from being violated or despised,

> we say that everyone ought, as much as possible,
> to hold the ministers of the Word and elders of the church
> in special esteem, because of the work they do,
> and be at peace with them,
> without grumbling, quarreling, or fighting.[12]

While a Reformed worldview, even in the sixteenth century, would recoil at the idea of a clerical class, there is a sense here both that bearing an office in the church requires a special kind of person and that bearing an office makes one special. These people are to be respected "for the sake of the offices they bear,"[13] as the Liturgy said until the twenty-first century. Beginning with the Articles of Dort (1619)[14] the constitutions of the denomination refer to many things that office bearers shall and shall not do, but also say, in each case, that "the office of (minister, elder, deacon, or professor of theology) is to..." before listing specifics. While these could be described as functions of the job, as certain aspects of each are listed in the successive versions of the government, they are, instead, referred to as part of the nature of the offices themselves, while also making it clear that each office is

---

[12] Belgic Confession, article 31. It is important to note that, in this era in the Netherlands, the office of deacon, while necessary in every congregation, was not part of the consistory, as governance was not part of their office. The American churches added deacons to the consistory owing to the relatively small size of American congregations and the small number of elders. See Allan J. Janssen, *Constitutional Theology: Notes on the Book of Church Order of the Reformed Church in America*, The Historical Series of the Reformed Church in America 33 (Grand Rapids, MI: Eerdmans, 2000), 16.

[13] "Liturgy for the Ordination and Installation of Elders and Deacons" (1987).

[14] Cited in Edward Tanjore Corwin, *A Digest of Constitutional and Synodical Legislation of the Reformed Church in America* (New York: Board of Publication of the Reformed Church in America, 1906), viii-lxxxvii.

something to which someone must be called, by God and by the church, freely recognizing God's call. The charter of the Reformed Dutch Church of New York makes it clear that there were some jobs—such as clerk, schoolmaster, bell ringer, and sexton—which may be filled in the church but which are not offices.[15] The "Articles of Union" of 1771 began the "Church-Order" with the statement, "For the Maintenance of good order in the Church of Christ, it is necessary that there should be certain Offices, Assemblies, Supervision of Doctrine, Sacraments and Customs, together with Christian Discipline."[16] Note that, again, we do not see a reference to people working in offices or people fulfilling certain jobs or responsibilities, but of the offices themselves existing as part of what constitutes a church.

Another understanding of the office that was transplanted from the Netherlands was that office-bearers needed to be prepared. In terms of deacons and elders, whose service was primarily in local congregations—and, prior to World War II, usually in the same local congregation for all of their lives—that formation was generally more informal. As John W. Beardslee, III, liked to point out, the preparation of elders and deacons happened around the Sunday dinner table: boys would hear their fathers, grandfathers, and uncles talking about that morning's sermon, what was going on in the consistory—with those no longer on active consistory offering their opinions and experience to those actively serving—and would learn by exposure how those offices functioned in that particular community.[17]

For ministers of the Word and sacrament—and, by extension, professors of theology—who had ministries to the whole church, the whole church took up a role in their formation. As early as the Articles of Union, provision was made for professors of theology chosen by the General Synod, even if it took a dozen years for the first concrete steps to be taken and a generation more for the theological seminary to take a shape familiar to modern eyes.[18] Indeed, until 1850, theological education was not simply a program in which the Reformed Church

---

[15] Cited in Hugh Hastings, ed., *Ecclesiastical Records of the State of New York*, vol. 2 (Albany, NY: James B. Lyon, State Printer, 1901), 1153 (hereafter *ERNY*).
[16] *ERNY*, vol. VI, 4218.
[17] Cited in James Hart Brumm, *Proclaiming the Good News in the Valley: A History of Grahamsville Reformed Church, 1844-1994* (New Brunswick, NJ: Historical Society of the Reformed Church in America, 1994). Young girls would not be formed for ministry by these congregations until late in the twentieth century.
[18] John W. Coakley, *New Brunswick Theological Seminary: An Illustrated History, 1784–2014*, The Historical Series of the Reformed Church in America 83 (Grand Rapids, MI: Eerdmans, 2014), 2-6.

had an interest, but a constituent part of who it was,[19] with that work being primarily achieved in a seminary, where students were off by themselves, not interacting much with the life of the larger church or the world, not even preaching in churches,[20] so that their energies might be devoted to formation for ministry.

This language regarding office and the received practices implied a lot, but said very little directly about the nature of office, especially not as it was synonymous with or distinct from function. Moreover, it was brought over from the continental Reformed tradition into the RCA with very little critical reflection; there was no discussion in the church about the meaning of "office": offices simply were. And so, as the RCA settled itself into the established American milieu of the late-nineteenth century, it defined "office" in more American terms, where the office was not something that existed before the office-bearer and continued to exist after him (or her, but it would have been an exclusively male domain in this era), nor as something that exists in concord—or *endracht*, a term important to the Dutch Reformed—with the other offices to support the body of Christ. The understanding influenced by U.S.-style democracy seems to have been "office" as a conduit for representation of the will of the body. In his essay "The Resemblance of its Ecclesiastical Polity to That of Our Country,"[21] William Mabon likens the office of minister to that of U.S. senators and elders to members of the House of Representatives, the former being an "upper" house and the latter a "lower" one, and praises the changeable nature of consistories—he must have been unaware of the self-replacing life terms provided by the Collegiate Church charter—as allowing "the introduction, from time to time of many of her sons into the duties and privileges of Church [sic] office; also, of securing the best talent for her services, and of relieving herself from officers who may be found, upon experience, unsuited to the work." All of this aids the church "in providing immediate representatives of the mind of the constituency for the time being."[22] Ideas of office-bearers being called by God and representing not the congregation's will but the divine will to the congregation seem to be absent. And it is interesting to note that

---

[19] Coakley, *New Brunswick Theological Seminary: An Illustrated History*, 26.
[20] Coakley, *New Brunswick Theological Seminary: An Illustrated History*, 16–17.
[21] Discourse XXII in *Centennial Discourses of the Reformed (Dutch) Church in America* (New York: Board of Publication of the Reformed Church in America, 1877). This is a collection of essays and lectures delivered by RCA ministers in celebration of the U.S. centennial in 1876.
[22] *Centennial Discourses*, 547.

this change in how office is expressed comes within a generation of the change in the understanding of the status of the seminary.

With the coming of the twentieth century came an increasing understanding of office as a set of functions. William Demarest, in his classic volume *Notes on the Constitution of the Reformed Church in America*, wrote about the possibility that the offices were fluid: "In the view of the church they have no sacred completion."[23] While this seems consistent with the idea of a church ever being reformed, it is clearly disconnected from the biblical roots of the offices mentioned above and from Calvin's reasoning for the offices that the church should maintain.

But Demarest took it a step further: "While the presence of officers is necessary for the proper functioning of the body and their presence is called for at once and always wherever a church exists, it cannot be said that a body without them is necessarily no church."[24] His logic was that, according to the Liturgy of 1906 and the church order of the time, a church was organized before elders and deacons were elected, and, therefore, that congregation was a church without offices represented in it. Still, it is a considerable logical distance from the sixteenth-century notion that offices are necessary for the function of the church to this idea that the church has always done things that way and it kind of works out.

The move toward a functional understanding of office reached its apotheosis in the Commission on Theology's response to the 1962 General Synod president's report, a 1968 paper on "The Nature of Ministry."[25] Part of the concern seems to arise from worries that the specialization of professional ministry had resulted in "the loss of the biblical viewpoint that all Christians are functioning, ministering members of a living body"—it was a concern about enabling the whole body. Another part seems to be a concern about power and equality: "there are more and more who bear rule in local judicatories who have no relation to local congregations." The most poignant concern was that "[m]any pastors, caught in the grip of crippling institutionalism, feel a deep sense of guilt for the failure to devote themselves to the tasks to which they feel called." Finally, there was a concern that the "institution" of professional ministry "places greater import on 'rights

---

[23] William Demarest, *Notes on the Constitution of the Reformed Church in America* (New Brunswick, NJ: New Brunswick Theological Seminary, 1928, 1944), 10.
[24] Demarest, *Notes on the Constitution*, 10.
[25] "The Nature of Ministry," in Cook, *The Church Speaks*, 115-23, 211.

and privileges' than upon responsible service to God and man."[26] This report, while having implications for all offices, focused on the office of minister. It saw Calvin's understanding of office as being primarily *munus*—function—and blamed "Protestant scholasticism" for making the concepts of the offices "sacrosanct—indelible and inviolable."[27] Proceeding from this perspective, and from a belief that "[t]he conception of ordination which is prevalent among us seems to be one of status and privilege"[28]—even though no data or even anecdotal evidence is cited as a basis for that belief—the paper concludes "the offices must be viewed as ecclesiastical functions ... All ministries outside the structure of the church which are not functions of her judicatories, or which are not principally aimed at the equipment of the church for her mission, should not be considered as functions of an office, but as part of the common ministry."[29] The paper goes on to speak of "commissioning" to a specific ministry, only for "as long as that service is continued,"[30] the elimination of ecclesiastical honorifics, and "a general de-emphasis on the rights and privileges of this office (minister of the Word), and a re-emphasis on the responsibilities and opportunities for service."[31]

By 1978, issues before the synod and changes in the membership of the Commission on Theology brought that commission to the decision that "the 'functional' view of ministry articulated in the 1968 report of the commission to General Synod needs to be reexamined."[32] The resultant paper, presented to the General Synod of 1980,[33] argued against either a purely functional view of office or one devoid of function, saying "the biblical evidence does not justify either of the two extremes."[34] It went on to define offices as "gifts of the Holy Spirit to the church" and, while acknowledging that "[o]ffices are as functional as any other ministry," insisted that they "have distinctive functions and other characteristics which distinguish them from the ministry which is common to the whole church."[35]

---

[26] "The Nature of Ministry," 115.
[27] "The Nature of Ministry," 117.
[28] "The Nature of Ministry," 120.
[29] "The Nature of Ministry," 121.
[30] "The Nature of Ministry," 122.
[31] "The Nature of Ministry," 123.
[32] *MGS* 1978, 240.
[33] "The Nature of Ecclesiastical Office and Ministry," in Cook, *The Church Speaks*, 124–36.
[34] "The Nature of Ecclesiastical Office and Ministry," 125.
[35] "The Nature of Ecclesiastical Office and Ministry," 128.

> Offices are those universally-recognized and continuing ministries within the church which differ from other ministries common to the fellowship. They are divinely appointed to represent, interpret, and proclaim the gospel of God's grace in Jesus Christ through the generations, and in so doing, to govern the church authoritatively by his grace and according to his purposes.[36]

This led the commission to state explicitly something that had previously been implied: "The offices...stand in a complementary and necessary relation to each other."[37] And that became a challenge: "We urge upon the church renewed attention to the complementarity of the offices. No one office is sufficient to represent the fullness of Christ or to communicate the fullness of the gospel of his grace."[38] In this paper, the Commission on Theology gives the RCA some of the first explicit statements of the nature of office that was implied in the sixteenth through eighteenth centuries.

> No one office stands above any other office, and by the same token, the offices should not be confused or intermingled. The deacon should not be burdened with the work of the elder, nor the elder with that of the minister, lest the full representing of Christ to the church and the mission of the church to the world be seriously diminished.
>
> We believe it is warranted by the Scriptures and fully consonant with our Reformed theology to affirm that there is a calling and a ministry which is characteristic and requisite of all believers. We also affirm a further calling and ministry addressed to some in the church for the equipping of the whole church. The latter, which we call offices, are distinguished in addition by the act of ordination and the laying on of hands.[39]

While the 1980 General Synod approved this paper, it was distributed with the 1968 report, which was considered to be "foundational."[40] Thus the RCA was presented with two somewhat contradictory views of office, espoused within a dozen years of each other, which, it would seem, were to be held in tension. Even those who

---

[36] "The Nature of Ecclesiastical Office and Ministry," 128.
[37] "The Nature of Ecclesiastical Office and Ministry," 130.
[38] "The Nature of Ecclesiastical Office and Ministry," 132.
[39] "The Nature of Ecclesiastical Office and Ministry," 132.
[40] Cook, *The Church Speaks*, 114.

argued for a higher view of office and a more complete exploration of what the offices could do, as Paul Fries did in his study "Faithful Consistories,"[41] acknowledged "those who question the role of the offices in the congregations of the Reformed Church in America have good reason to do so."[42] As the role of commissioned pastor has been created in the RCA, it is established as something between the established offices. Even strong advocates of the new role acknowledge that it "lies somewhere in between the two offices which require substantial education and deep spiritual maturity, minister and General Synod professor, and the two offices which are perceived by most as volunteer and obtained by a simple election process, elder and deacon."[43] While it seems to arise out of a functional view of ministry as laid out in the 1968 report, there is the argument that "we used the word 'pastor' rather than 'elder' to honor the training, credentials, and call of the individual and to make clear his or her authority and responsibility."[44] This seems to contradict some of the very egalitarianism that the 1968 report professed, while also potentially confusing the offices in a way that the 1980 report warned against. This is problematic, as it seems to both ignore our existing, albeit conflicted, understandings of office and to further muddy the waters. It has been pointed out that "those of us who serve the church in the area of its order are culpable for having allowed the church to use language that does not accurately describe who we are."[45] Indeed, the General Synod of 2014 sent to the classes an amendment allowing commissioned pastors to supervise consistories,[46] which arguably denies the "complementarity of the offices" affirmed by the 1980 General Synod in approving the Commission on Theology paper. The act of holding these two views of office in tension appears to be accomplished only with difficulty, if at all.

This paper is trying very hard to avoid arguing for a correct definition of "office," instead seeking to define where we are and how our previous understandings have led us to this place. As the RCA

---

[41] Paul Fries, "Faithful Consistories," Reformed Church in America, 2001, www.rca.org/resources/faithful-consistories.

[42] Paul Fries, "Coordinates for a Theology of Office: Footnotes for an Emerging Narrative," *Reformed Review* 56, no. 3 (2003): 203.

[43] Carol Mutch, "A Response to 'Elder-Pastors and Deacon-Evangelists' and 'From Maintenance to Ministry,'" *Reformed Review* 56, no. 3 (2003): 259.

[44] Mutch, "A Response," 260.

[45] Carol Myers, "Response to 'Reaction or Prescription' and 'Charism and Office,'" *Reformed Review* 56, no. 3 (2003): 231.

[46] MGS 2014, 239.

explores new forms of ministry, however, it seems that a consensus is needed on what office means and how, if two conflicting views are to be maintained, they might both be honored. Shifting the church's ecclesiology by legislation rather than discussion and reflection seems to be fraught with potentials for misunderstanding and error. It should be noted that the last time such a conversation actually addressed the place of office in the life of the church was during the Great Synod of Dort, where it took place over a period of months, not hours. This might be difficult in the structures of the RCA as they are currently employed. Several scholars and other faithful people have, in recent years, been advocating creative ways to live out the offices that are consistent with our ecclesiology.[47] Before taking too many steps to create ministries and roles that redefine our understandings of office, we might do well to employ just such creativity.

---

[47] In addition to those resources cited above, readers might also look at Allan J. Janssen, *Kingdom, Office, and Church: A Study of A. A. van Ruler's Doctrine of Ecclesiastical Office*, The Historical Series of the Reformed Church in America 53 (Grand Rapids, MI: Eerdmans, 2006).

CHAPTER 4

A Look at the History of the Term "Bounds," Particularly Pertaining to Classes[1]

The 2018 General Synod, in approving a recommendation from the professorate, voted,

> To request the Commission on Church Order, Commission on History, and Commission on Theology to offer its interpretation of the word "bounds" in the Book of Church Order, defining specifically its relationship to geographic boundaries and its implications for ethnic classes, for report back to the 2019 General Synod.[2]

This request, of course, does not arise from a vacuum, but from the very real experiences not only of the Classis of the City, the first true non-geographic classis in the RCA, but even more significantly, to the creation of the Classis of the Americas, a classis that understands its bounds to be based primarily upon ethnicity.[3] Certainly this is not the

---

[1] *Minutes of General Synod* (hereafter *MGS*) 2019 (New York: Reformed Church Press, 2019), 260–65.
[2] *MGS* 2018, 322.
[3] *MGS* 2018, 321.

only time that classes based on ethnicity have been proposed, but it is the first time that it has been effected. Indeed, as we seek to lean into our future as a multiracial and multiethnic church communion, these are deep questions with which we must wrestle. These are theological questions and they are, truly, existential questions.

Each of the commissions looks with a different focus. There is what can be done and what ought to be done. The Commissions on Church Order and Theology have this as their charge. The Commission on History is called to chronicle and analyze the history of the use of the term "bounds" and the ways in which classes have been understood. It is to this end that the commission offers this paper.

Spiritual Geography in the Bible

Already in the beginning of the biblical narrative, we are able to gain a sense of the importance of place. Genesis tells us that God planted a garden, and the waters that watered the garden branched out into four rivers that gave life to the world that they knew. The narratives, particularly in the Old Testament, are replete with geographic references. God called Abram when he resided in Haran. Abram was told by God to walk the length and breadth of the land that God had promised to him and his descendants. The people of God were enslaved in Egypt (and Egypt was also the place to which the holy family fled Herod's sword). Throughout the entire biblical narrative, there is the importance of the land and the Temple. These were not only locations on a map, places to perform rites or space on which to live. These were deeply imbedded into the spirituality of the ancient people. Even in the exile, we can see an intentionality of place, even (or perhaps especially) when it is hard to understand. "[S]eek the welfare of the city where I have sent you into exile," we read in Jeremiah, "and pray to the Lord on its behalf, for in its welfare you will find your welfare" (Jeremiah 29:7). Even in exile, there is an importance of place, of geography, of locality.

The Reformed Church in the Netherlands was formed, interestingly enough, not in the Netherlands but in Germany. It was in Emden that, in 1571, the first Dutch Reformed synod was convened, and this synod marks the beginning of a national Reformed church for the Dutch people. This synod was convened outside of the Lowlands precisely because the Reformed were persecuted and had to be underground. A synod could not be convened on Dutch soil, and so the East Frisian port city of Emden, across the Dollard Bay from the Province of Groningen, was chosen for this synod.

It was at this synod that all the various underground Reformed churches were to form themselves into classes, as described in the Acts of the Synod of Emden.[4] These classes were geographical. Part of this was practicality: there were Dutch Reformed exile communities in both Germany and England, as well as the fact that proximity was important to be able to do the needed work of a classis in the time. This would be the framework from which the Dutch Reformed would structure the church.

Nearly 50 years later, another national synod was convened, this one in the Dutch city of Dordrecht, and, among other things, this synod prepared a new church order, of which our *Book of Church Order* is a direct descendant.

The Dutch Reformed Come to the Americas

Not quite ten years later, the Dutch West India Company sent the first Dutch Reformed minister to the North American colonies. Immediately upon his arrival, he ordained an elder and a deacon, forming a complete consistory so that a church could be founded. For the first 154 years of the Reformed Church's existence in North America, there were no classes, as it was an extension of the Classis of Amsterdam. This was a difficult arrangement, partly because of the distance and difficulty of communication, partly because ministers needed to be educated and licensed in the Netherlands, but also because the Classis of Amsterdam lived a very different contextual reality than the churches in North America. The drive for independence from the Classis of Amsterdam wasn't solely about the education of ministers; it was largely about a church trying to find itself in a very different reality from the Netherlands. By the time what was to become the Reformed Church in America was made independent, New Netherland had been New York and New Jersey—and parts of Pennsylvania and Delaware—for a hundred years, the primary language spoken was English, as they lived not under the flag of the Dutch Republic but the Union Jack of Great Britain. Part of the deep and painful division in the years leading up to the Plan of Union was the growing autonomy of the colonial Reformed churches, and eventually the church split into two camps: those who advocated subordination to the Classis of Amsterdam and

---

[4] Acts of the Synod of Emden, Arts. 10–12, trans. Richard de Ridder, in *The Church Orders of the Sixteenth Century Reformed Churches of the Netherlands, Together with Their Social, Political, and Ecclesiastical Context*, ed. Richard de Ridder, Peter H. Jonker, and Leonard Verduin (Grand Rapids, MI: Calvin Theological Seminary, 1987).

those who advocated for independence. While there were concessions made by both parties in the Plan of Union, it effected the independence of the Reformed Protestant Dutch Church in North America, which could now govern itself within its own contextual reality.

Neighboring, District, and Bounds

This Church Order of Dort of 1619 does not speak of bounds, but it speaks of the classis as being "composed of *neighbouring* churches."[5] Additionally, the particular synods are composed of "four or more *neighbouring* Classes."[6] The word "neighbouring," here, gives a clear implication of geography, that is, a classis is composed of churches that are close to one another, neighbors to one another, churches that share a similar contextual existence, churches that have been planted near one another.

After the conclusion of the Revolutionary War, the Reformed Church eventually adopted and published its Constitution. The Synod adopted the Church Order of Dort of 1619, but also appended the Explanatory Articles, which sought to help apply the Dortian order to the new context. Article XXXVIII of the Explanatory Articles defines the classis as "all the Ministers, with each an Elder, and one Elder from every vacant congregation within a particular *district.*"[7]

The term "bounds" is, itself, somewhat peculiar. While it would be nice if the church order clearly defined the terms that it uses, this is not the case here. From the minutes of the General Synod in the years surrounding its introduction into the order, one can see many uses of the term "bounds" in various contexts. We may tend to think of "bounds" primarily in the context of classes or regional synods, but the use of the term "bounds" was quite liberal in the early nineteenth century. Indeed, local churches had bounds, classes had bounds, particular synods had bounds, and the general synod had bounds as well.

Some instances more clearly refer, at least in the background, to geography. Indeed, in referring to the North Carolina Classis of the German Reformed Church in 1855, the minutes of the General Synod report: "its bounds extend one hundred and forty miles in one direction

---

[5] The Church Order of Dort, 1619, Art. XLI, trans. Edward Tanjore Corwin, in Edward Tanjore Corwin, *A Digest of Constitutional and Synodical Legislation of the Reformed Church in America* (New York: Board of Publication of the Reformed Church in America, 1906), xlvii–l, emphasis added.

[6] The Church Order of Dort, 1619, Art. XLVII, in Corwin, *Digest*, lvi, emphasis added.

[7] Corwin, *Digest*, xlviii, emphasis added.

..."[8] This gives the impression that bounds has to do with a geographic existence, that is, its bounds expand over a geographic area which is served by churches, rather than churches which compose the bounds. Furthermore, in other contexts, " ... the Classis within whose bounds it is located."[9] Again, the use of "located" gives a sense of geographic locality, as if an academy could be located within the geographic area that is overseen by the classis.

Long Island Appeal

Of note, however, is a complaint by the Classis of Long Island against the Particular Synod of New York to the General Synod of 1830. The Bushwick church was transferred by the Particular Synod of New York from the Classis of Long Island to the South Classis of New York. The record shows that there was some displeasure on the part of the Bushwick church, and they requested the particular synod to transfer them, which was done. The Classis of Long Island complained and argued that,

> ... prejudices, preference, like or dislike, were never designed as a rule for the guidance of Particular Synod, in the organization or enlargement of these courts. But on the contrary, it is found in all such cases that no other rule has been recognized than geographical contiguity ...[10]

The classis, in the complaint, goes on to cite the aforementioned articles from Dort and the Explanatory Articles and the words "neighboring" and "district." Similarly, the argument given was that the action of the particular synod violated the understanding of bounds. "Providence seems to have fixed their natural bounds, and to have drawn a broad watery line [the East River] between them and the churches in the city."[11]

In the complaint, the classis also looked beyond.

> If the ecclesiastical relations of one, two, or three congregations can be changed at pleasure, or upon some fancied grievance, upon the same principle the relation of all the churches, throughout our whole connexion, may be immediately broken up, and our

---

[8] *MGS* 1855, 535.
[9] *MGS* 1846, 89.
[10] *MGS* 1830, 272.
[11] *MGS* 1830, 273.

Classes become nothing more than mere voluntary associations. Every tie which now binds the Church in harmony together, and gives weight to her authority, will be completely severed; and every thing like order will soon come to an end.[12]

We do not know the substance of the synod's deliberation, nor can we know the exact reasons that the synod voted to sustain the complaint. However, it was presumably not disconnected from the classical argument in this case. While this one case does not constitute binding precedent (indeed, binding precedent is not something that exists in the RCA), it does provide an example of a strong assertion of the geography of classical bounds, and this case is worth considering when we speak of bounds.

Classes of Pleasant Prairie and Germania

There are two peculiar classes that are worth noting and briefly discussing, because they have bearing on the issues of bounds and ethnicity. The Classis of Germania is often cited as an example of an affinity, or even a non-geographic, classis in the history of the RCA. This analysis is not exactly wrong, but not quite right, either.

There is a strong German Reformed component to the RCA as well. Many of these Germans came from East Friesland—whose principal city is Emden—and two vestiges of this heritage are the Classes of Pleasant Prairie and Germania. The former still exists, the latter has since been disbanded. Neither truly non-geographic, nor necessarily affinity, they were linguistically-bound classes, at least in origin.

With the influx of German Reformed churches and the growing need for pastors for these churches, a German-language classis was formed: the Classis of Pleasant Prairie. This is not entirely without precedent. The Netherlands was a land of two languages: Dutch and Walloon (French). The early church orders allowed for separate consistories, classes, and particular synods for Dutch- and Walloon-speaking people. However, it also recommended that in cities where there are Dutch and Walloon churches the ministers and elders gather monthly to maintain unity and assist one another.[13]

The Classis of Pleasant Prairie was formed in 1892 with several churches in Illinois and Iowa. The existing churches came from the Classis of Wisconsin and Iowa, and others were started after the

---

[12] *MGS* 1830, 275.
[13] For example, see Church Order of Dort, 1619, Arts. LI and LII, in Corwin, *Digest*, lviii.

establishment of the classis. While Pleasant Prairie was not strictly geographic, it was also not non-geographic, as all of these churches were in a similar geographic region. It was not so much an ethnic classis; it was a linguistic classis. That is, it was not a classis for ethnic Germans; it was a classis for German-speaking people. The differences seem small, but they are not insignificant.

The Classis of Germania came into existence in 1915 and was formed with 17 churches, all from the Classis of Pleasant Prairie. By this time, Pleasant Prairie was some 39 churches, covering an area of over 700 miles.[14] The churches in the Classis of Germania were German-speaking congregations in the Iowa-Minnesota-South Dakota juncture. Like Pleasant Prairie, it was not truly non-geographic, because they were in the same geographic area; it was not necessarily an ethnic classis, but it was a linguistic one.

These two classes also had different life cycles. Pleasant Prairie remains a classis to this day, though they no longer speak German, nor do they necessarily identify as German. As the people, and the congregations, became more Americanized, they blended in with those in the region, the majority of whom descended from northern Europeans. While its origin was as a linguistically-bound classis, it did not remain one. The Classis of Germania no longer exists: its name was changed to the Classis of North Central in 1964, and it was dissolved by the Particular Synod of the West in 1969, its churches distributed among neighboring classes.

Conclusion

To be sure, there are many considerations and many angles from which to seek to understand the meaning of bounds, both what has been, what can be, and what ought to be. Historically speaking, the understanding of "bounds" has always included a geographic component. Some of this may be convenience, particularly without modern technologies that aid in communication. However, as the complaint of the Classis of Long Island displays, it is not simply a matter of convenience. There is also a sense of place as a theological concept, a type of spiritual geography.

The professorate identified two presenting concerns; namely, non-geographic classes based on some affinity and classes that are defined

---

[14] Schnucker, George. "The German Element in the Reformed Church in America," in *Tercentenary Studies: A Record of Beginnings* (New York: General Synod of the Reformed Church in America, 1928), 439.

by race or ethnicity but where the churches are also geographically proximate.

Historically speaking, both of these are new developments for the RCA. Ethnic classes are not something that the denomination has embraced, though linguistic bounds are something that reach to our earliest roots.

Ultimately, the question that we will have to face is this: Do we learn to live with each other because God has planted us together, or do we gather based on a particular affinity?

SECTION 2: THE GENERAL SYNOD

CHAPTER 5

To Collect and Preserve[1]

To fulfill the responsibilities charged to it by the General Synod, as well as to keep faith with all future generations who will ask questions of this era and all previous eras, the Commission on History submitted to the General Synod Executive Committee in January the following program proposal which, as this report was being written, was awaiting consideration by the full General Synod Executive Committee and General Program Council for possible recommendation to this Synod:

I. The Necessary Components of an Adequate Archives

To meet the responsibilities assigned to it by the General synod of 1966 and qualify as an active, responsible program of historic preservation, an archives for the Reformed Church should have at least the following characteristics:
- A. There should be a safe and spacious deposit and storage facility.
- B. There should be responsible servicing of archival materials. This should include at least the following persons:
  1. Archivist—this person should, on a full-time basis:
     a. Be trained in the most recent theory and skills.
     b. Be responsible for a complete program of records management/archival preservation.
        i. Search out and collect relevant materials.

---

[1] *Minutes of General Synod* 1977 (Grand Rapids, MI: Dickinson Bros., 1977), 239–42.

ii. Select materials for preservation.
iii. Organize, process, and preserve materials.
iv. Oversee reference and research use of materials.
2. Secretarial and servicing assistance.
A. There should be a regular, ongoing program of active procuring/collecting of historical materials relevant to the life and work of the Reformed Church.
B. There should be a systematic program of microfilming all documents of continuing historical significance where the loss of the original would limit or impair future understanding of Reformed Church history,
C. There should be a systematic program of oral history by means of which denominational leaders could record for posterity their own reflections on their careers, influence and experience.
D. There should be a regular program for the publication of significant studies which explore the history of the Reformed Church (especially those studies which make use of the denominational archives).
E. There should be firm direction and control of the program. The commission on History would seem best equipped to oversee program development. The personnel suggested in this proposal should be related to the denominational staff in a means appropriate to their responsibilities and consistent with current denominational practice. The exact details of these relationships are left to the discretion of the General Synod Executive Committee.

II. The Present Situation

As a denomination, we now have ten years of experience with the present organizational format for the Commission on History. We have made certain advances and experienced considerable success. Our archives has gained world-wide reputation and has served as the database for a significant amount of research. An honest appraisal of our present situation would indicate:

A. The denomination does have a deposit facility for its archives. Since 1841, when a single case was installed in the consistory rooms of the Collegiate Church, through 1876, when the archives was first moved to the Gardner A. Sage Library and down to

the present time, a physical place, with some permanence, has been assigned to the archives. The present facility is, however, of extremely limited capacity.
1. It now provides no room for storage of additional materials.
2. It has no provision for protecting fragile paper materials from:
   a. Fire
   b. Water damage
   c. Acidification
   d. Theft
3. It has almost no space for material preparation, technical processing or research use of materials.

A. The denomination does have an extremely dedicated staff of three persons working diligently, but caught in the impossible task of attempting to carry out a very diverse program on a part-time basis.
   1. Integration of a dynamic archival program is impossible.
   2. Oversight of research and control of materials must be carried on at a level far below what would be recognized as a professional minimum.
B. As a denomination we have been able to carry on NO regular, active, program of searching out and collecting additional historical materials. No program of records management has ever been instituted, so there is little direct control over which materials ought to be/are preserved and which can be destroyed.
C. Our denominational program of microfilming, which began in the late 1960's with budgets of more than $1,000 and which saw vast amounts of irreplaceable records microfilmed, has now slowed to a mere trickle of production.
D. A program for recording oral history has been funded (at $2,800 per year by the General Program Council), but to this point no person has been in a position to give the program direction or impetus.
E. During the last eight years the one genuine bright spot in the program of the Commission on History has been its publishing record. Four significant works on the life and work of the RCA are now available to church members and to others interested in our history.

F. The Commission has sought to give responsible oversight to the varied aspects of the present program. We have, however, found ourselves increasingly frustrated by the fragmentary nature of our present program—a program which is, at best, the result of organizational evolution, circumstance and the vagaries of part-time attention. Perhaps it should be here recognized that our present stipend for our archivist would entitle us to about 1/20 of a person's time and abilities. On this slim basis much has been accomplished, but there still remains at least 19/20 to be done.

III. Proposed Program

In order to correct the shortcomings of our present program (for which no individual nor the Commission can or should be held responsible) and in order to provide the kind of records management/ archival preservation program that the past, the present and the future of our denomination deserve, we have recommended that the General Synod Executive committee approve and recommend to the General Program Council as well as to the church-at-large the following phased-development toward an archival program of high quality. The GSEC Is considering our recommendation at this time.

Phase I

A. Steps should be taken immediately to obtain for the denomination the services of a highly-skilled, professionally experienced archivist ON A FULL-TIME BASIS.
   1. This person should be charged with denominational responsibility for:
      a. A program of records management to assist the General Program council, the Extension Foundation, the Editorial council of the CHURCH HERALD, the Board of Pensions and any other board, agency council or commission of the church. A properly designed program of records management effectively administered can improve operational efficiency, reduce reference/ research time, assure availability of significant data and document the present for future historians.
      b. The organization, care and general oversight of the archives of the Reformed Church.

c. An active program of searching out, acquiring, photocopying or microfilming records, documents, etc., which have relevance to the history of the RCA.
  2. This person should have the following qualifications:
     a. Should be trained in the best of current archival methods.
     b. Should be alert to the principles of records management.
     c. Should have some experience In an archives similar to that which we hope ours will become.
     d. Should be sensitive to and knowledgeable in the history and character of the RCA.
 B. Steps should be taken Immediately to provide an assistant (or assistants equal to one full-time person) who shall facilitate the work of the archivist and assist In the organization and care of the archival materials.

This archival program will provide an efficient records management service both for the materials of General Synod and its churches as well as the General Program Council, It Is estimated that presently the General Program Council functions generate approximately 60 percent of our archival materials while General Synod, Particular Synods, Classes and congregations produce the remaining 40 percent. Expenses would be shared accordingly. It should be noted that General Synod is already committed to cover Commission expenses, office expenses, and microfilming costs. In 1976 the General Program council committed itself to cover expenses of an oral history program up to $2,800 (none of which was spent due to lack of personnel to manage the program). The Commission is also currently funded to cover present part-time salaries. The above financial support would, of course, be integrated with the new archival program.

   Phase II

During the second phase of this proposed program, the Commission on History will attempt to establish a Reformed Church Historical Association. This association would have as its purpose:
  1. The appointment, in each of our congregations, classes and synods, of one person who would serve as historian/archivist, with the responsibility of documenting the history of that church, classis, etc.

2. The provision of a means by which persons interested in our history can be better informed about that history, exchange information with each other and contribute creatively to our knowledge of our past.
3. The education of our church (primarily through the work of the archivist) in the preservation of historical materials and the means by which they can be used to facilitate the ongoing life and work of congregations, classes and the church-at-large.

Phase III

After phases one and two have stabilized themselves (perhaps by 1981) this proposal envisions an increased commitment of denominational funding for the purpose of enlarged programs of:
1. Records management
2. Microfilming
3. Preservation and restoration of documents.

Phase IV

Finally, we envision a phase four, in which we can begin to formulate plans for enlarged and improved physical facilities to house our archives. There may be advantage in exploring the possibility of some decentralization. Perhaps deposit facilities can be related to the various regional centers. Both New Brunswick seminary and western seminary are in the process of planning new or expanded library buildings. These plans may hold possibilities for our denominational archives which should be examined.

CHAPTER 6

Historical Development of the President's Report[1]

The current form of the President's Report, with its substantial length and at times numerous recommendations, is a relatively recent phenomenon in the life of the RCA.

The first State of Religion report was given in 1812. Each year General Synod appointed a small committee to review the State of Religion reports from the particular synods. Consistories submitted these reports to classes, which sent them to the particular synod. During most of the nineteenth century the committees prepared reports to General Synod that were relatively brief (three to five pages) and focused upon statistical analysis. Were there more people received on confession this year than last year? Did the gains (confessions and certificate/transfers in) exceed the losses (deaths, dismissals, transfers out)? Did the rate of growth exceed that of the previous year? How many children were in catechism and Sunday school classes?

The reports also tried to capture the current state of religion in a more qualitative way, and for this they depended on the reports from consistories and classes. Some consistories reported revival activity

1   *Minutes of General Synod* 2004 (New York: Reformed Church Press, 2004), 101-05.

and large increases in membership. In other years churches lamented that the showers of God's grace had not fallen upon them in any great measure. While the RCA grew steadily throughout the nineteenth century, the reports often criticized the church for spiritual weakness if the rate of growth did not exceed that of the previous year.

The State of Religion reports made about fifty resolutions between 1831 and 1930. One-fifth of these dealt with the statistical reports, which were notoriously incomplete and sometimes inaccurate. The committee repeatedly urged congregations, classes, and particular synods to turn in their reports and include all the numbers. Several resolutions expressed gratitude to God for grace and mercy. Other resolutions expressed concern for church practice. The Heidelberg Catechism should be regularly preached and taught. Children should be baptized, educated, and prayed for. Giving should increase. The 1872 report included resolutions about the need for temperance and Sabbath observance, but that was the only example of attention to social and moral issues.

In 1884, the past president of General Synod began to chair the committee which prepared the State of Religion report. Soon the committee dropped out. The reports from the particular synods were to be sent in advance of the meeting to allow time to prepare a thorough report, but there was often only a brief time between the meetings of the particular synod and the General Synod. Until about 1920 the reports commented on the meaning of the statistics, although presidents occasionally reflected on the broader culture and the challenges it presented for religious life.

The content of the reports shifted in the 1920s from numbers to a more interpretive analysis of trends and patterns in the RCA. In 1922 the president noted some of the differences in the particular synods and concluded that there were two types of RCA churches: those ministering to a homogeneous ethnic group and those ministering in a very diverse community. Different methods were necessary and churches should charitably accept such differences. In 1927 the president examined the causes for a drop in giving and members. He observed that rural areas were already experiencing problems with crops, and in the East, changing industrial conditions were changing the neighborhoods around RCA churches.

The reports varied in their quality. Some presidents made some very good suggestions. But they rarely put them into the form of a resolution, and therefore their perceptive comments were not likely to go beyond the room where the speech was delivered. In 1931 President Milton Hoffman suggested that his speech be referred to a five-person committee. The committee then made six recommendations based on the proposals in Hoffman's report. During the next several decades a few presidents made recommendations. Others did not, and occasionally the committee did so for them. On two occasions, in 1952 and 1955, David Van Strien and Gerrit VanderLugt gave very thoughtful addresses about RCA identity, but made no recommendations. Van Strien's committee thanked him for the splendid report. VanderLugt's committee drafted recommendations that deal with two minor parts of the report, but failed to translate the substance into recommendations. Unfortunately, some of the best reports were the most difficult to translate into specific recommendations.

The role of the president expanded significantly in the twentieth century. In 1913 President William Bruce suggested that synod supply money for the president to take a trip. He went to Michigan several times for meetings. In 1925 William Bancroft Hill traveled to the Midwest in hopes of easing some of the East-West tensions that had developed in the RCA. In 1939 President J. Harvey Murphy reported that he traveled thirteen thousand miles and gave one hundred twelve addresses. He also gave one of the longest reports to date! In 1943 Joseph Sizoo said that he had conversations with five hundred ministers in small groups. In 1958 Howard Schade traveled twenty-five thousand miles to study the church so that his report would be relevant. The office of president had grown significantly to include attending a variety of meetings, visiting, and speaking. In 1960 Howard Hageman visited every area of the church but one. In 1962 Norman Thomas mentioned his two-month trip to India, the Middle East, and the Sudan. Most presidents after him took a trip to an international mission site, and frequently traveled to Brewton, Annville, and the Native American missions as well. The presidency had moved a long way from the nineteenth-century pattern of being elected simply to preside at one meeting of the General Synod. RCA polity had not kept up with the changes, however, and there was little formal guidance, structure, or authority for the office of president.

One of the reasons for the growing power and influence of the presidency was that the RCA lacked any kind of coherent and unified staff structure during most of these years. During the nineteenth and first half of the twentieth century, the life of the RCA was primarily shaped by three boards: Foreign Missions, Domestic Missions, and Education. The executives in charge of these boards were usually extremely gifted, committed, and charismatic figures. Each board was made up of about fifty people (usually Easterners for ease of travel to meetings) who were passionately devoted to their cause. The boards raised their own money and were quite successful. There was no structure in place which conducted the work of the General Synod in between meetings. There was no structure which coordinated or mediated between the sometimes competing goals and claims of the boards. The president began to function as the central voice of the RCA in part because there was no other person who served in that role. The RCA did have a half-time stated clerk for much of the twentieth century, but he really was a clerk whose primary roles were managing records, distributing funds, and planning the General Synod meeting.

In the 1940s, the presidents regularly expressed a need for some kind of central governing structure. This may have seemed important in part because other denominations were becoming more bureaucratically organized, but they saw that as the RCA grew it could not continue to function with a structure designed in 1792 for a small regional church. In 1937 Raymond Clee proposed the formation of a President's Cabinet, a combination of staff and clergy that would inspire spiritual life and coordinate the work of the boards. This met for a few years and then disbanded. Some people criticized it as too staff dominated. In 1943 Joseph Sizoo proposed a committee of fifteen of the best minds of the church (including women) that would deal with planning, publications, the post-war world, and pastoral transitions. He hoped it would "end our drifting." A special committee was formed to draft a specific plan, but synod defeated it by two votes. Several presidents made similar proposals in the next fifteen years, culminating in the period from 1958 to 1960 when three presidents spoke eloquently about the need for better administration of the RCA. In 1961 president Henry Bast met with the two past-presidents, Marion DeVelder and Howard Hageman, and the vice president, Norman Thomas. They drafted a specific plan for a three-year trial of the General Synod Executive Council (GSEC), which Bast proposed in his address and synod approved. The GSEC proved to be essential to the life and growth of the RCA during the next decade. Marion DeVelder was also called in 1961 to be the full-time stated clerk (later general secretary) of the RCA.

These transitions in staff and structure did not diminish the role of the president. In the 1960s the presidents became more involved in the life of the RCA, spent more time traveling and attending meetings, and presented longer reports with more recommendations. In 1968 the title was officially changed to "The President's Report" since it was clear that the content had relatively little to do with the state of religion. Their recommendations were very diverse. Some dealt with programmatic issues and encouraged more evangelism, prayer, or outreach. Then, as now, it was difficult to oppose a recommendation to pray! A number of recommendations dealt with ministers' well-being, support, salaries, and continuing education. Some presidents proposed a fairly significant change in the life of the denomination, such as the way it elects the vice president of synod, or the way it deals with students who go to non-RCA seminaries, or the funding of the denominational magazine. A few offered as many as seventeen recommendations on a variety of topics. Others offered one. At times the interests of the presidents could lead the church in multiple directions. One year, for example, the president suggested the RCA develop extensive relationships with churches in Hungary. The next president suggested extensive relationships with churches in the Caribbean. Some presidents identified an issue that was causing anxiety in the church, as when Leonard Kalkwarf asked in 1984, "What is the glue that holds us together?" A multi-year study of denominational identify followed.

What happened to all these recommendations? Some were enthusiastically approved by synod, enacted, and continue to have an impact. Others were approved but languished in a committee. Some were soundly defeated by General Synod. Some proposals were initially dismissed, but after several other presidents raised a similar issue, synod took action. Some of the most creative ideas received minimal attention. Occasionally a relatively minor proposal consumed a great deal of the church's time and energy. Many of the proposals demanded a great deal of the staff. The presidents frequently added to the staff workload but rarely took anything away. Occasionally an excellent recommendation was referred to a body that was not able to deal with it. For example, the General Synod Council (GSC) was given a recommendation asking that it examine the historical, cultural, and structural barriers to the leadership of women, but that is not the kind of research GSC members generally do. That recommendation might have been better referred to the Commission for Women or the Commission on Theology.

Since the 1990s presidents have frequently identified one major issue that shapes all of their recommendations. These themes have included inclusivity, communication, equipping laity, outreach, leadership, Reformed theology, congregations as mission stations, the statement of mission and vision, use of the four ordained offices, lay ministries, prayer, and the Holy Spirit. They are all important topics and all useful to the church. But each presidential recommendation usually requires money or significant staff time or more meetings. Financial and human resources are limited. The church cannot do everything. How should the church decide which of all these good ideas it should pursue? And who determines that some of these ideas may not be the most useful for the future of the church? How does the church welcome and implement creative new ideas without going in a thousand different directions? How does the church determine which initially difficult and daunting ideas might be good for the RCA, and which are inconsistent with our identity, or simply impossible to carry out?

Most recommendations appear in the General Synod workbook and delegates have the opportunity to study and discuss them in advance. Presidential recommendations are presented on Friday, discussed in advisory committees on Saturday, and voted on early the next week. This may not give the General Synod adequate time for discernment, especially given the quantity of business synod must consider.

Any changes to the *Book of Church Order* (*BCO*) or the bylaws require two readings, and *BCO* changes require classis approval. It seems inconsistent to allow major programmatic changes to occur simply based on the recommendation of one person without more thorough and extended discussion than synod can provide.

The Commission on History believes that the recommendations arising out of the presidents' reports deserve sustained attention by the commissions and agencies of the RCA. The General Synod has at times found it difficult to say no to a popular and well-intentioned president. Recommendations have been approved even though they might take the church in a very different direction, or demand financial and human resources which are already stretched to the limit. Excellent recommendations sometimes do not receive the attention they deserve. Weak recommendations sometimes get too much attention. The style of these reports has evolved more by tradition and habit than out of any reflection on their place in our polity, and the changes need to be recognized by our church order. Automatically referring the presidential recommendations to the appropriate commission or agency would give the RCA more time and space to consider what actions should be taken in light of its history, its identity, and its goals for the future.

CHAPTER 7

An Examination of Historical Precedent for Setting RCA Policy[1]

According to the *Book of Church Order* (*BCO*):

The General Synod alone shall determine denominational policy. It may delegate the formulation of policy to committees, boards, or other agencies.[2]

The question, however, involves a larger question: does the nature of this General Synod authority reflect the "teaching" or the "position" of the entire church, and are all members of the RCA, boards, and seminaries subject to those General Synod positions?

Throughout RCA history, the issue of General Synod authority in policy matters has been the subject of debate and decision. It has always been clear that the denomination as a whole made authoritative decisions by making changes in the Constitution. Or, to say it another way, constitutional changes have always reflected authoritative decisions

---

[1] *Minutes of General Synod* (hereafter *MGS*) 2007 (New York: Reformed Church Press, 2007), 306–10.
[2] *Book of Church Order*, 2005 ed. (New York: Reformed Church Press, 2005), I.IV.2.4.

made by the entire body, and such changes are constitutionally binding on the body.

The larger debate, however, has had to do with the relationship of the General Synod to lower assemblies (regional synods, classes, and congregations). In reviewing that relationship in its historical context, it becomes clear that the denomination has intentionally refrained from granting authority to the General Synod to establish the definitive teaching of the church.

The *Explanatory Articles* of 1792 say of the General Synod that it is "the last resort in all questions, which relate to the government, peace, and unity of the church. To this is committed the superintending the interests of religion, the maintaining harmony, and faithfully preserving the Churches in the principles and practices of religion."[3] How did it function as the "last resort"? The 1876 version of the Constitution was bound with a document entitled "Digest of the Synod Legislation." The General Synod had declared itself on a number of matters.

There was, for instance, the highly mooted question of the marriage of a man to his wife's sister. Was this permitted? After wrestling with this issue for a number of years, the synod concluded:

> Whereas the rule prohibiting the marriage of a man with his deceased wife's sister is found only in resolutions passed by General Synod at its previous sessions, and not in the Constitution of the Reformed Church; and whereas a majority of the Classes have reported against such rule, therefor,
>
> *Resolved*, That all resolutions which may have been passed by the General Synod, forbidding a man to marry his deceased wife's sister, be and hereby are rescinded.

The synod was clear; the "rule" in question had only been found in synodical resolutions and therefore did not have constitutional authority. It was, thus, rescinded.

The General Synod's authority in matters of policy was clearly in evidence in the controversial question of whether members of congregations could also be Freemasons, as addressed in the previous paper. The Synod of 1880's resolution included the following paragraphs:

---

[3] Explanatory Articles of 1792, Article LI, in Edward Tanjore Corwin, *A Digest of Constitutional and Synodical Legislation of the Reformed Church in America* (New York: Board of Publication of the Reformed Church in America, 1906), lviii.

Resolved, That while, on the ex parte evidence of the memorials now before it, this Synod cannot properly give its official testimony for or against Free Masonry and other oath-bound secret societies; and while it holds as sacred the indefeasible rights of all its ministers and members to their individual conscientious convictions and liberty of speech and action, subject only to their prior loyalty to Christ and to His Church, yet it hereby declares that no communicant member, and no minister of the Reformed Church in America ought to unite with or to remain in any society or institution, whither secret or open, whose principles and practices are anti-Christian, or contrary to the faith, and practice of the Church to which he belongs.

Resolved, That This Synod solemnly believes and declares that any system of religion or morals whose tendency is to hide our Saviour, or to supplant the religion of which He is the founder, should receive no countenance from His professed followers; and furthermore, that no humane, benevolent or philanthropic, or reforming agency in this world can take the place of the Church of Our Lord and Saviour Jesus Christ, whose principle is to "do good unto all men, but specially to them that are of the household of faith," and, therefore, that who belong to this Church are in duty bound to give it the pre-eminence over all orders or institutions, and to promote to the utmost of their powers its unity, peace and prosperity, and especially its great charities and philanthropies.[4]

The General Synod needed to emphasize its position in response to the "Christian Reformed Church in the Netherlands" criticizing the General Synod for allowing church members to become Free Masons. The synod was clear that it had expressed its opinion. At the same time the synod quoted itself in its response when it stated that "it [the General Synod] has neither the power nor the disposition to interfere with the prerogatives of the lower bodies in the exercise of discipline, except only in the manner prescribed by the Constitution."[5]

General Synod, then, had the authority to act as a synod, but not to enjoin the lesser assemblies to act in concert with the synod's decision itself. The synod could and did act in judicial matters and could and did act as it proposed changes in the Constitution itself.

---

[4] *MGS* 1880, 533-36.
[5] *MGS* 1889, 838-39. The issues of both temperance and Sabbath observance were also resolved in a similar manner. See Corwin, *Digest*, 101-03.

The clause on "policy," inserted in the article that set out the responsibilities of the General Synod, found its way into the church order as the church was reorganizing its administrative structure. By 1959, the General Synod had begun to think in terms of an "Executive Council." This would bring some coordination to a denomination that was structured through its various boards (e.g., the Board of Education or the Board of World Mission). It is instructive to listen to the committee's reasons for the method of choosing members of the various boards. They included:

> That the boards were subsidiary corporations of the GS and as such should be chosen by the GS and not by lower judicatories.

The designation of board members by area judicatories "would be an open invitation for the emergence of local pressure which would be most unfortunate."[6]

There was a clear concern to avoid the balkanization of the church and to maintain the clear responsibility of the boards to the General Synod itself. No board was to be autonomous, and so, one might propose, speak (or make policy) on behalf of the entire church.

This concern becomes clearer as one moves further into the report. The committee stated that the activities of the denomination are conducted by both 1) "ecclesiastical structure"— boards of elders, consistory, classes, and synods and 2) outside the structure as in educational institutions, the pension system, and the missionary program.

The boards, the report stated, are separate corporations but subsidiary to and responsible to the General Synod. They are designed as agencies to perform "those functions which lie outside the normal operation of the churches...The problem arises from the fact that in the recent years we have been attempting to use some of these subsidiary corporations to perform functions that lie inside the ecclesiastical structure. For example, the work of the Board of Domestic Missions in church extension seems to conflict with the constitutional prerogatives of the several Classes, and that of the Board of Education in the area of Christian education of children, youth and adults overlaps the normal functions of local churches, Classes and Particular Synods." Furthermore, "...the use of subsidiary corporations to exercise functions inside the ecclesiastical structure does not work satisfactorily because

---

[6] *MGS* 1959, 144.

there is no official line of communication with or responsibility to the churches, Classes and Particular Synods where these functions normally and constitutionally belong."[7]

It appears fair to conclude, then, that the restriction to the establishment of policy was directed toward the boards in an attempt to give coherence to the actions of the General Synod. It was an assertion of the authority of the General Synod in matters of a denominational nature.

Of what such matters consists may be a matter of some contention. Herewith are three instances, two from papers or policies enacted by the synod and one from a judicial matter before the synod, that turned on the question of the General Synod's sole authority to establish policy.

In 1988, the General Synod's Commission on Theology offered a paper on the question of the nature of the saving action of Jesus Christ. The synod prepared to endorse the paper as faithful to the teaching of Scripture and of the Standards of the RCA. However, as the synod prepared to take action, the motion was amended to read that the paper be "provisionally recognized" as faithful to the teaching of Scripture, etc.[8] The synod proceeded to vote the endorsement with amendment. Two matters are to be noted. First, the action on the paper itself referred beyond itself to both Scripture and the Standards. It was not the synod itself, but the true constitutional authority—Scripture and the Standards through which Scripture is understood—that was placed at center. Second, by adding the phrase "provisionally recognized" the synod backed away from any pretense of magisterial authority.

A second, perhaps clearer, instance of the General Synod's approach to policy is found in an earlier paper and subsequent actions placed before the synod in 1985 by the Christian Action Commission. That commission had been instructed to advise the synod on whether and how the synod should invest its moneys with corporations involved in the production of nuclear weapons. After taking up the paper itself, the synod voted:

> **R-2**
> To direct the Office of Finance to reduce investments to the minimum level necessary to initiate shareholder resolutions in those companies in the nuclear weapons industry that meet the following criteria.

---

[7] *MGS* 1959, 145.
[8] *MGS* 1988, 464.

It also voted:

R-3

To instruct the General Program Council, in consultation with the General Secretary and the Office of Finance, to appoint a Peacemaking Investment Panel whose task shall include:

a. advice and counsel to the RCA Office of Finance and the Advisory Committee on Investments; and other RCA agencies, assemblies, institutions, and individual members;

b. dialogue with corporate management in the nuclear weapons industry;

c. initiation of shareholder resolutions;

d. assessment of the corporate response to the church's peacemaking witness.

R-4

To instruct the Office of Social Witness to distribute the study "The Church's Peace Witness in US Corporate Economy" to RCA agencies, assemblies, congregations, and related institutions for study, urging them to join this peacemaking witness.

R-5

To instruct the Office of Social Witness to provide information concerning corporations involved in the nuclear weapons industry to RCA agencies, assemblies, congregations, and related institutions and to inform them of shareholder activities designated to further the church's peacemaking witness.[9]

Here the General Synod was very clear. It took a policy action that had direct consequences: how the General Synod would invest its own funds. However, it made no move to direct any other assembly or body within the church to take a similar action. The synod would urge other bodies to do so. Indeed, it established a small committee that carried out just that task. The synod's own authority, however, was limited in this instance.

In 1992, a complaint was brought against the Synod of the Mid-Atlantics, charging that it took a position on abortion contrary to

---

[9] *MGS* 1985, 63–64.

that of the General Synod. The complainants argued that the regional synod violated that section of the Book of Church Order that reserved policy to the General Synod. The regional synod had, so they argued, established a contrary policy.

The Judicial Business Commission agreed with the complainants and asserted that contrary to the General Synod, a regional synod has no "explicit grant of policy-making authority." Or more correctly, that what policy-making authority a regional synod may possess "must yield to that of the General Synod in cases of even potential conflict."[10]

It appears that the General Synod has augured a shift in its authority at this point. What had been a matter of policy in relation to the various boards and agencies now is understood as policy with relation to the lesser assemblies. The General Synod no longer retains the caution that it must leave to its lower bodies the freedom appropriate to their ecclesiastical status.

---

[10] *MGS* 1992, 104.

CHAPTER 8

History of Funding for General Synod[1]

The General Synod of 2018 voted "[t]o direct the general secretary to authorize and fund" the new position of coordinator of interreligious relations.[2] Further, this position is to be funded from reserves rather than through an assessment.[3] In this discussion, several concerns were voiced about the level of assessment and the rate at which the assessment increases. Your commission thinks it beneficial to briefly chronicle the history of funding for the General Synod.

The purpose of this short paper is largely two-fold: to understand the variety of ways the General Synod and the denominational program has been funded and to understand the origin of assessments and the development thereof. Our current assessment process is a way that we have funded the denominational program, but it is certainly not the only way. And our assessment process was not so much a process that was designed but one that developed relatively organically.

---

[1] *Minutes of General Synod* (hereafter *MGS*) 2019 (New York: Reformed Church Press, 2019) 265-72
[2] *MGS* 2018, 97.
[3] *MGS* 2018, 65-66.

Colonial Funding Practices

The traditional approach to funding the church in the Netherlands was that the support of the clergy was raised from the property that had belonged to the Catholic church with local government supplements. This practice transferred to New Amsterdam, as salaries were paid by the Dutch West India Company. When the English took over in 1664, they decreed that each parish should pay for the support of the minister, which was a difficult idea for the Dutch settlers to accept. Johannes Megapolensis, in a letter to the Classis of Amsterdam in 1669, remarked that,

> On Sundays we have many hearers. People crowd into the church, and apparently like the sermon; but most of the listeners are not inclined to contribute to the support and salary of the preacher. They seem to desire, that we should live upon air and not upon produce.[4]

The early American practice of raising funds for the local church developed through the rental or sale of pews. This annual payment provided for the support of the minister and for the construction of the church building. Offerings were occasionally taken for the care of the poor in the community, but generally, these offerings were not the rule.

Independence and New Responsibilities

With independence from the Classis of Amsterdam, two main areas of fundraising arose: mission work and the professorate. With the growth and the projected growth of the new republic, new churches were needed in these new settlements and communities. As a result, the General Synod made the first denominational appeal for funds in 1788, when it requested the classes to make voluntary collections from their churches for the purposes of church extension.[5] "With these moneys ministers were sent out on horseback tours, thro [sic] central and western New York and Canada."[6] The General Synod continued to ask for funds through voluntary collections taken at the churches on particular Sundays throughout the year.

---

[4] Hugh Hastings, ed., *Ecclesiastical Records of the State of New York*, vol. 1 (Albany, NY: James B. Lyon, State Printer, 1901), 602.
[5] *MGS* 1788, 181.
[6] Edward Tanjore Corwin, *A Digest of Constitutional and Synodical Legislation of the Reformed Church in America* (New York: Board of Publication of the Reformed Church in America, 1906), 149.

The Professorial Fund was established to attempt to raise sufficient funds for the theological professorate. Despite the good intentions, such a fund was never sufficient, nor was it able to adequately support the professorate, often causing hardship to the professors and embarrassment to the synod.[7] Money was raised by subscriptions, though these were often not sufficient or went unpaid. As the General Synod was not yet incorporated, the funds were held by the trustees of Queens College. In 1815, the General Synod determined to hold its own money for the professorate and the establishment of the Permanent Fund, which was merged with the Professorial Fund in 1828.[8]

Collection for denominational funds was increased in 1812 when the General Synod "enjoined" churches to make collections for theological education, one half of which was to support the professor, and the other half of which was to fund the procuring of a library and support students who lacked the necessary financial means to pay for their education.[9] Congregations were encouraged to contribute to the Professorial Fund, although without universal success. The concern about this from the synod can be seen in the order for classes to publish the names of churches that had not contributed to the Professorial Fund.[10] This continued through the 1820s as synod recommended other mission efforts for collections but had no power to force contributions. As early as 1830, the General Synod suggested a per-communicant-member offering of 25 cents for the support of the theological seminary.[11]

Development of the Assessment Process

In 1818, the General Synod established a Contingent Fund to defray costs of the General Synod itself, such as, "the expenses of the stated and permanent Clerks, the expenses of stationery, the doorkeeper, &c. while the Synod is in session, and the expenses incurred by the Committees of Synod in the discharge of the duties of their commissions..." This Contingent Fund would repay money that was borrowed from the Missionary Fund to cover these expenses and to pay for these expenses in the future.[12] This fund would be supplied

[7] Edward Tanjore Corwin, *Manual of the Reformed Church in America*, 4th ed. (New York: Board of Publication of the Reformed Church in America, 1902), 163-69.
[8] Corwin, *Digest*, 552-53.
[9] MGS 1812, 429.
[10] MGS 1815, 43.
[11] $0.25 in 1830 is equivalent to nearly $7 today.
[12] MGS 1818, 53.

by the "proceeds of the copy right [sic] of the Constitution" and "the profits arising from printing the minutes of Synod…" Additionally, the requests made to the churches for the support of mission work would also include financial support of the Contingent Fund,[13] though later they would unlink these appeals.[14]

The fund did not receive overwhelming support, and the Minutes of General Synod are peppered with encouragements to classes to increase support for this fund. Despite this, though, this fund was able to meet the expenses that required payment from it. However, through the 1840s, the General Synod was having difficulty supporting the professorate and in meeting the costs of running the synod (e.g., printing minutes, office supplies, etc.), and in 1847, it was noted that the synod had to resort to loans in order to meet its obligations.[15] In order to discharge the debt as well as support the expenses of the synod, it was proposed in 1848 to "assign each Classis a sum proportionate to the number and ability of its churches, to be paid by them … to the Treasurer of the General Synod."[16] Here is the first time that we see an assigning of a proportionate sum to classes.

By 1850, the matter became quite serious, and the issue of the synodal debt was again brought to the fore, reporting that the debt reported in the previous year still existed. The Board of Direction reported that although a request for a collection was made, as was the custom, it had been "almost entirely overlooked by the churches." Again the board recalled the plan to proportionally distribute the financial burden among the classes.[17] The report of the professorate also addressed the dire financial straits.

> The debt of the Synod, it is noticed with regret, has not been paid, and this must become a more painful matter under the ordinary action of Synod. It is easy to vote in our annual sessions the payment of moneys, but if our plans for securing the necessary sums in the hands of the Treasurer are not carried out faithfully, it is plain our difficulties must increase…The debt is one of the whole church, and it is equitable and just that it should be parcelled among all sections, to be provided for according to their ability.[18]

[13] *MGS* 1818, 61.
[14] *MGS* 1821, 13-15.
[15] *MGS* 1847, 116–17.
[16] *MGS* 1848, 277.
[17] *MGS* 1850, 22.
[18] *MGS* 1850, 91.

The General Synod voted to carry out the plan that was proposed in 1848 in order to eliminate the debt and provide sufficient funds for the General Synod.

> Resolved, That a Committee, consisting of one from each Classis here represented, be appointed to assess upon each Classis a sum proportionate to the number and ability of the churches, and sufficient to meet the existing debt and the contingent expenses of the Synod.[19]

In addition to this, the ministers and congregations were urged to take up collections to support the work of the mission boards, the education board, and the Sabbath School union. It was clear that this assessment was not to eliminate the usual manner of collections and subscriptions for the support of the mission of the broader church.

Beginning in 1857, the shortfalls in synodal revenue were assessed among the classes. This was met with payments, refusals to pay, and complaints.[20] In 1862, it was reported that the income was still insufficient to meet the financial obligations of the synod, primarily the salaries of the professorate and the contingent expenses of the synod. The classes were not contributing, and the synod noted the difficulties with determining a just distribution between the classes. To this end, the General Synod decided to assess the particular synods and allow the particular synods to determine the distribution. There were three particular synods at the time: Albany, New York, and Chicago. The Particular Synod of Chicago was not assessed, and the financial burden that they owed was divided between the Eastern synods, with New York bearing two-thirds of it and Albany bearing one-third.[21]

The process became more solidified in 1868, when an addition was made to the responsibilities of the Board of Direction so that they would, each year, propose financial measures as they deem necessary for the expenses of the church.[22] It was in this year that the assessment began to look much closer to what we experience today.

> These expenses are connected with the existence of the Synod. The Synod exists for the defence of ecclesiastical rights...The poorest farmer in the distant West is as certain of obtaining a candid

---

[19] *MGS* 1850, 105.
[20] *MGS* 1864, 474.
[21] *MGS* 1862, 189-90.
[22] *MGS* 1868, 411.

hearing as the wealthiest Elder from the metropolis. Should not the farmer in return for this equal protection pay a full share of the trifling expense which arises from the existence of the judicatory. [sic] Two cents a member will secure the necessary amount.

And with this, there were two significant changes. The first is that the treasurer of the General Synod would assess classes rather than particular synods; and the second is that the number of communicant members would serve as the basis for this assessment.[23]

It should also be noted that during this time, the General Synod had relatively few expenses. The delegates paid for their own travel expenses and requested reimbursement from their classes. An exception was the delegates from the Midwest, for whom the General Synod covered travel expenses. But apart from the expenses of the synod itself and the support of the professors, there were few program expenses that the General Synod itself generated.

Move Toward United Program and Funding Strategy

Over time, the denominational program grew. The program, however, was overseen by a federation of quasi-independent boards that raised their own funds and were not assessed. Toward the beginning of the twentieth century, there was a drive for efficiency to enhance effectiveness. All the boards, together, reported to the General Synod requesting there to be a, more or less, unified denominational program; together, more can be done in the service of Christ. But this united approach was not just in terms of the program itself, but also in terms of funding the denominational program.[24] The Progress Campaign, as it was called, was to end after five years but was eventually continued by the General Synod as the Progress Council.[25]

The Progress Council was discontinued after a new campaign was begun, and the synod felt that having a single campaign before the church was more beneficial.[26] This also meant that the boards were often competing for resources. In order to avoid this, in 1946, the General Synod adopted a united appeal approach, that the boards would work together to raise funds—the United Advance.[27] One might be able to see

---

[23] *MGS* 1868, 413.
[24] *MGS* 1918, 535-41.
[25] *MGS* 1932, 187.
[26] *MGS* 1937, 129.
[27] Marvin D. Hoff, *Structures for Mission*, The Historical Series of the Reformed Church in America 14 (Grand Rapids, MI: Eerdmans, 1985).

the United Advance as the next step from the Progress Council. What can be seen here, as well, is not only a desire for a more unified system of funding, but also a more structured and unified denominational program, a way to bring together and coordinate the program of the denomination. "The United Advance was the most comprehensive evangelism and stewardship program ever to be undertaken by the Reformed Church in America."[28]

The United Advance presented its final report in 1949, noting that while it did not quite meet its goal, it was very successful. One of the recommendations was to consider a more permanent united approach to the denominational program. To this end, a committee was established and instructed to report back the following year.[29] In 1950, the committee affirmed the importance of, among others, a "clearly defined, coordinated program."[30] To this end, the Stewardship Council was created to help with the coordination of the denominational program by gathering, among others, representatives from the several boards.[31] This continued through the 1950s during a time of growth and expansion of services to local churches.

Finally, in 1968, the consolidation of the denominational program was completed when three boards merged with the Stewardship Council to create the General Program Council (GPC).[32]

Funding Church and Program

As we have already mentioned, assessments were not the first denomination-wide fundraising efforts. The Reformed Church has had a long history of raising money for many purposes, particularly benevolent purposes. The raising of funds for benevolent purposes began to be more organized when, in 1867, the General Synod ordered the formation of a committee "to devise and report to General Synod ... some scheme for securing, if possible, generous and systematic contributions from all our Churches to all our Benevolent Boards."[33] The committee reported back the following year and recommended, among other things, that "it is the duty of every settled minister, and of every consistory where there is no settled minister, to see to it that the

---

[28] Hoff, *Structures for Mission*, 83.
[29] *MGS* 1949, 181-91.
[30] *MGS* 1950, 182.
[31] *MGS* 1952, 156.
[32] *MGS* 1968, 141.
[33] *MGS* 1867, 286.

collections ordered by Synod are regularly taken up in the Churches under their care."[34] Additionally, a question was added to the annual constitutional inquiry to inquire into whether or not collections were taken for the boards of the General Synod. And so it is not only that churches themselves ought to support benevolent causes on their own, but that they are to join with other Reformed churches in unity of purpose and action for benevolent purposes, as well. Indeed, the denomination was urged to support denominational benevolent causes first.[35]

Benevolent funds were gathered either in collections or in the form of what we might today call askings. The General Synod doesn't tax for them, but expects churches to give generously, just as it asks people to do the same. While there has been some difficulty with a strict line between benevolence and administration,[36] there has been a distinction between those things which are to be assessed, and those things which are to be solicited via special offerings or other forms of giving.

For most of the history of assessments, the General Synod assessed for church purposes, not program purposes. That is, the General Synod assessed classes for costs of the synod functioning as an assembly of the church. This meant that costs such as the stated clerk, commissions, contributions to ecumenical organizations, and the like were assessed, because these were part of the General Synod as an assembly of the church. Much of the program, however, was undertaken by a federation of quasi-independent boards. These boards were subsidiary corporations of the General Synod, and they had their own staff and their own budgets and ran their own programs. The various assemblies of the church, then, could decide what programs to support and how.

At the same time that the denominational program was consolidating, the General Synod, in responding to calls throughout the church, sought to determine what were benevolent funds and what were operational funds—benevolent contributions being voluntary and operational funds being assessed. The problem that the synod noted, however, was that there is not a clear demarcation between benevolent and operational, since benevolent programs require operational

---

[34] *MGS* 1868, 504.
[35] *MGS* 1936, 548-49.
[36] *MGS* 1968, 179.

support.³⁷ In the State of Religion report in 1972, the president of General Synod called for a consultation that would, among other things, find a way to provide financial strength to the denominational program and to maintain the balance between assessment and benevolence.³⁸ In 1973, definitions were offered for assessment, asking, and offering. Administrative costs (synodical staff salaries, travel and meeting expenses, office expenses, etc.) are assessed whereas denominational "programs of ministry and mission" are non-assessed, "including the costs of implementing such programs." The funding of staff services was determined by the General Synod Executive Committee (GSEC) and the GPC for their respective costs.³⁹

Increasing Assessments and Growing

Through the 1980s and 1990s, assessments increased as did the complaints, proposals of alternate strategies, and attempts to curb assessment increases. Between 1980 and 1994, there were no less than 27 overtures expressing concern over assessment increases—and several of these were sent by more than one classis. Following up on a referral from 1980 to consider additional funding strategies in addition to assessments (instead of assessing for program), the General Synod of 1981 established a program called "support share." Support share was an attempt to encourage churches to give based upon income rather than membership. When it was first introduced, it was recommended to give three percent of income for congregational purposes which would be divided between Christian discipleship, church planting, and development. This was not an assessment, but rather, was an encouragement to the churches for their support.⁴⁰

This was also a time in which the GPC was seeking to address funding problems and was running a deficit. The deficit led to a number of staff positions being eliminated from the budget, and it was noted that the GPC would require a ten percent increase in funds over the next year in order to eliminate further deficits, and support shares were again urged to the churches.⁴¹ The following year, the deficit was reversed and support shares did not make another appearance. However, in 1987,

---

[37] *MGS* 1968, 179-80; *MGS* 1972, 91.
[38] *MGS* 1972, 279.
[39] *MGS* 1973, 124.
[40] *MGS* 1981, 254-55.
[41] *MGS* 1982, 225-27.

the General Synod voted to establish an assessment to maintain the staffing of the GPC.[42] The following year, there were 11 overtures from a number of classes asking to rescind the assessment program, to consider alternatives to assessments, and to ask the General Synod to account for how assessment dollars are spent. The synod denied nearly all the overtures, but it did call for the GSEC to prepare a study on the strain of assessments on financially struggling churches.[43]

The reasons provided against assessments presented in the overtures during the 1980s fall into a few general arguments. The primary concern was for the traditional means of voluntary giving for benevolences. Assessments violated that tradition. Seen as a form of taxation, in fact a "regressive" tax, it was natural that human beings would rebel against being told what they must do. Such mandatory giving restricts congregational control and weakens the levels of accountability.[44]

Related to this "traditional" argument was the argument that "forced" giving weakens us, while voluntary giving, cheerfully done, leads to a spiritual enthusiasm. A per capita tax makes for spiritual discomfort. Such a situation may cause giving not to be the result of a cheerful heart.

Finally, the third argument related to the power and control over the classes and congregations held by General Synod. Assessments would continue to grow as more "worthy" programs were added that were in financial trouble. Such a situation would mean that synod would have complete control over classes and congregations as congregations lost the freedom to contribute based on the merit and value of individual programs.[45]

Each of these overtures was denied by the General Synod. Regularly arguments were presented that indicated the importance of the program for the church and the necessity for funding it. The overtures gradually shifted from an opposition to assessments to that of controlling the increase of assessments and providing assistance for economically troubled churches. As the RCA entered the 1990s and began to assess for *The Church Herald*, and especially to send it to every household and fund it through assessments,[46] the concern was

---

[42] *MGS* 1987, 265.
[43] *MGS* 1988, 345–53.
[44] *MGS* 1980, 225.
[45] *MGS* 1988, 345–53.
[46] *MGS* 1992, 198–99.

not so much against assessments as it was for the rate of increase of assessments.

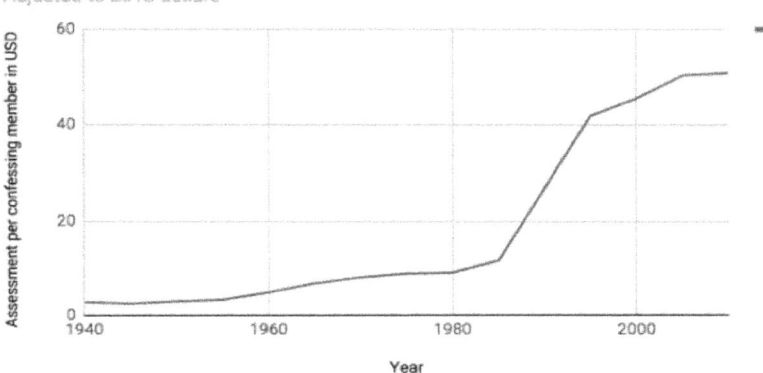

Conclusion

The General Synod had funding structures, plans, and strategies that adapted organically to the needs of the denomination. The General Synod has a long history of assessing the narrower assemblies (synods and classes) for operational costs, though benevolence and program costs have long been supported by voluntary contributions. It is only recently that the General Synod has begun assessing for program purposes. It is because of the assessing for program purposes, and not simply operational purposes, that there has been such a significant increase in assessments. But, the General Synod began assessing for program because the churches and classes did not adequately fund the program aspects of the church that were, in appearances at least, desired by the church.

SECTION 3: BEING CHURCH

CHAPTER 9

A Historical Examination of the Relationship Among RCA Assemblies As Conceived in the Articles of Dort (1619) and the Explanatory Articles (1792)[1]

It is commonly accepted practice in biblical exegesis to work not only from the original languages of the Scriptures but from the oldest, most complete editions of those manuscripts available. As the RCA seeks to examine and redefine the structures of its various assemblies and the ways in which they relate to each other for the second time in less than a decade, it seems prudent to use a similar approach, to strip away the layers of accumulated changes to have a common view of the starting point.

The Rules of Church Government, Established in the National Synod, Held in Dordrecht in the Years 1618 and 1619 are also known, by virtue of Edward Tanjore Corwin's citation,[2] as the *Articles of Dort*, to distinguish them from the Canons of Dort which were written at the same Great Synod of Dort, convened in response to the Arminian controversy. The

---

[1] *Minutes of General Synod* (hereafter *MGS*) 2007 (New York: Reformed Church Press, 2007), 310-12.
[2] Edward Tanjore Corwin, *A Digest of Constitutional and Synodical Legislation of the Reformed Church in America* (New York: Board of Publication of the Reformed Church in America, 1906), x-lxxxvii.

laws of the province of North Holland required the New Netherland congregations—in the colony that became New York, New Jersey, and parts of Pennsylvania and Delaware—to follow those rules,[3] and so they did for 164 years.[4] In 1792, they were not so much supplanted as they were explained; John Henry Livingston, Dirck Romeyn, and Eilardus Westerlo were assigned by the Provisional Synod in 1788 to translate the Dort articles, and then proposed a completely new constitution,[5] but an extraordinary synod held in May of 1792 voted only to create a set of "articles in explanation" to adapt the existing constitution to the American situation.[6]

The order from Dort referred to a National Synod, particular synods, classes, and consistories, which remained much the same in the Explanatory Articles, except for a change in nomenclature to refer to a General Synod. The American church was not connected to the national government, nor could it reasonably pretend to have national scope; on the other hand, the Americans did not need to see themselves as having national boundaries. Relationships among the assemblies were very similar to what the modern RCA knows: the General Synod would create particular synods (which did not happen in the US until 1800[7]), particular synods would form classes, and classes had the authority to form and dissolve consistories. Consistories sent delegates to classes, and classes sent them to particular synods, but it was particular synods that chose delegates to the General Synod.[8]

This role of the particular synods may seem odd to us, but it made sense in light of the fact that the particular synods were designed to be the largest annual assembly. The General Synod, following the Dort pattern, was intended to meet only triennially.[9] While the General

---

[3] Daniel J. Meeter, *Meeting Each Other in Doctrine, Liturgy, and Government*, The Historical Series of the Reformed Church in America 24 (Grand Rapids, MI: Eerdmans, 1993), 31.
[4] The Plan of Union, which was adopted in 1772, did not replace the Dort Articles, even though it established a General Body and Particular Bodies in North America. Instead, it specifically reinforced Dort: "We adhere, in all things, to the constitution of the Netherlands Reformed Church, as the same was established in the Church Orders of the Synod of Dordrecht." See Meeter, *Meeting Each Other*, 33-34.
[5] Corwin, *Digest,* 160.
[6] *MGS* May 1792, 229.
[7] *MGS* 1800, 301-03.
[8] This was only true for the first few General Synods. After that, classes chose delegates whom the particular synods approved. Corwin, *Digest*, lx-lxii.
[9] Such a schedule commenced once particular synods were formed in 1800, creating a true General Synod, but the General Synod reverted to an annual schedule in 1813. See *MGS* 1812, 441; *MGS* 1813, 9. Ironically, in the Netherlands, the opposite

Synod was to be the body that maintained the theological professorate and the Constitution, the particular synods were to be the primary body dealing annually with the life of the classes and supporting their work.

An examination of the Minutes of the Particular Synod of New York gives some clue to how that relationship played out. While the particular synods had been created with only one mandate—to examine students of theology—New York promptly assigned this task to its classes,[10] and appointed *deputatis synodi*—synod deputies—from each classis to ensure the quality of examinations. This meant that, on an annual basis, at least, every classis was visited by ministers from one of its sisters, who reported back to the synod on how examinations were conducted and who, on occasion, made suggestions as to how classes might learn from one another.

During that first century of New York Synod's existence, the work of the deputies was but the tip of the dialogical iceberg. At the very first meeting, the synod appointed committees to review minutes from other particular synods and the General Synod, as well as state of religion reports from its own classes.[11] These discussions were very detailed and extensive. Fraternal delegates from other particular synods were in attendance,[12] and suggestions for how sister synods should deal with concerns before them would be freely exchanged, as would suggestions and ideas for challenges faced in the classes. The annual meetings were, in a real sense, town meetings, times for community sharing.

Nor was this sharing limited to classes and particular synods. In 1816, after the General Synod suggested that baptism should only be administered to children whose parents proved they possessed faith and piety, New York refused to pass the idea along to its classes, and instead responded to the General Synod that its notion was "contrary to the word of God and the standards and usages of the Reformed Dutch Church."[13] In later years of the century, the particular synod

---

happened: rather than meeting again in 1622, another national synod was not convened until 1816 (Meeter, *Meeting Each Other*, 80).

[10] See James Hart Brumm, "The Synod of New York Convened," in *Equipping the Saints: The Synod of New York, 1800–2000*, ed. James Hart Brumm, The Historical Series of the Reformed Church in America 35 (Grand Rapids, MI: Eerdmans, 2000), 4. New York Synod must not have been alone in this practice, as classical oversight of theological examinations becomes part of the Constitution in 1833. See Corwin, *Digest*, 485.

[11] *Minutes of the Particular Synod of New York* (hereafter referred to as *MPSNY*) 1800.

[12] At first, the only particular synods were New York and Albany, but others were formed over time.

[13] *MPSNY* 1816, 6.

would challenge the validity of General Synod assessments and refuse to pass them on to the classes.[14]

The return of General Synods to annual meetings, combined with the growth of staff for the General Synod and the expenses and territorial disputes that accompanied this saw these practices fade by the end of the nineteenth century; in 1898, the General Synod appointed the first committee to study whether or not particular synods were necessary or an encumbrance.[15] Nevertheless, there is clear evidence that the original conception of classes and synods in the Reformed Church in America was not hierarchical, but conversational. All of these bodies were intended for mutual support and accountability to advance the shared work of the gospel. The system was, evidently, envisioned with a parity of assemblies analogous to the parity of offices we still enjoy.

---

[14] For specific examples, see *MPSNY* 1864, 7, 53-54; *MPSNY* 1867, 5-6, 59-60; *MPSNY* 1868, 7-8, 66.

[15] *MGS* 1899, 496-502.

CHAPTER 10

Commissioned Pastors in the Reformed Church in America: A Historical and Contextual Survey[1]

In 2014, the General Synod voted to instruct the General Synod Council to consult, in part, with the Commission on History to:

- Detail the original purpose and subsequent history and evolution of the commissioned pastor in the life of the RCA.
- Explore the theological foundations of office in the RCA as they pertain to the commissioned pastor.
- Engage the relational tensions that the subject of commissioned pastors has produced in the church.[2]

The Commission on History has identified four categories relevant to this discussion that warrant further investigation for historical perspective and guidance. These categories are: comforters of the sick, dispensation/Approved Alternate Route, commissioned preaching elders, and commissioned pastors.

---

[1] *Minutes of General* Synod (hereafter *MGS*) 2015 (New York: Reformed Church Press, 2015), 197–203.
[2] *MGS* 2014, R-56, 267.

Comforters of the Sick[3]

The Reformed Church in America traces its history to 1628 with the arrival of the Rev. Jonas Michaeleus, the ordination of the first elder and deacon, and the organization of the first Reformed church in New Amsterdam. However, 1628 does not mark the beginning of ministry in New Netherland. Several years before, Bastiaen Krol and later Jan Huygens, two Ziekentroosters, or comforters of the sick, were sent to New Amsterdam to provide religious care for the faithful there who were not numerous enough to warrant a minister.[4]

The comforters of the sick provided a needed ministry presence to the Dutch colonies in the absence of ministers. A liturgical form was created for the comforters of the sick and consisted primarily of "consolatory texts of scripture."[5]

Shortly after arriving in New Netherland, Krol returned to Amsterdam to request a minister to be sent, as the colonists were desiring someone who could perform marriages and, considering the fact that women were pregnant, administer baptism. The consistory in Amsterdam determined that the population was not large enough, but gave Krol permission to perform marriages and baptize. He was to study and read the liturgical forms and if he was to deliver a sermon, he was "to read one from an accepted book of sermons written by Reformed theologians."[6] Although Krol was given an increased role within the colonies as a comforter of the sick, he was clearly not a replacement for a minister, as he was "specifically instructed not to interject any of his own words into either the liturgical formulas or into the sermons."[7]

The comforters of the sick, then, had a significant ministry to the Reformed in the Dutch colonies worldwide, and for our purposes, New Netherland. It is, however, important to bear in mind that the comforters of the sick were never intended to be a replacement or substitute for

---

[3] The Dutch words for this role were *Krankenbezoekers* and *Ziekentroosters*. "Strictly speaking, the former means a seeker out, or visitor of the sick—especially those overtaken suddenly by sickness; while the latter means a comforter of those who are very sick—especially when nearing their end. Practically, these two terms were used synonymously" (Hugh Hastings, ed., *Ecclesiastical Records of the State of New York*, vol. 1 [Albany, NY: James B. Lyon, State Printer, 1901], 46 [hereafter *ERNY*]).

[4] Gerald F. De Jong, *The Dutch Reformed Church in the American Colonies*, The Historical Series of the Reformed Church in America 5 (Grand Rapids, MI: Eerdmans, 1978).

[5] *ERNY*, 46.

[6] De Jong, *The Dutch Reformed Church*, 13.

[7] De Jong, *The Dutch Reformed Church*, 13.

ministers of the Word, but rather, were charged with helping the faithful with their spiritual needs in the absence of a minister. However, even as ministers began arriving in New Netherland, comforters of the sick continued to aid in the ministry to the colonists and "continued to be sent to New Netherland for forty or fifty years from 1626."[8]

Dispensation/Approved Alternate Route

The Reformed churches have always valued an educated ministry, and have required that candidates for the ministry undertake a course of studies prescribed by the church. However, the Reformed church has also understood that there may be some people gifted for ministry in extraordinary ways. Therefore, the Church Order of Dort included a provision for people who had not undertaken the required course of study, only if, "the best assurance be obtained of their singular talents, piety, humility, sobriety, good understanding, and discretion, together with the gifts of utterance." If the synod approved, the classis could examine them, and if found acceptable, they were to, "according to their proficiency... enjoin a course of private exercises; after which they shall be dealt with as shall be judged most conducive to edification."[9]

When the first constitution was adopted for the new independent Reformed Protestant Dutch Church in North America, the church order required that "no student can be admitted to a public examination before any Classis or Synod unless he shall produce a document under the hand and seal of a Professor of Theology, appointed by the General Synod."[10] This document was later referred to as a "professorial certificate."[11] However, to the General Synod were reserved "all regulations respecting any further term for study, or any particular dispensation, which peculiar circumstances may render necessary in the case of any students in Theology..."[12] Therefore, the earliest church order of the Reformed Church allowed for the General Synod to grant dispensations, that is, "permission to do something not strictly in accordance with ecclesiastical law."[13] It should be noted, however,

---

[8] *ERNY*, 48.
[9] Dort Article VIII, in Corwin, *Digest*, xvi.
[10] Explanatory Articles of 1792, Article XXIII, in Edward Tanjore Corwin, *A Digest of Constitutional and Synodical Legislation of the Reformed Church in America* (New York: Board of Publication of the Reformed Church in America, 1906),, xxvi.
[11] The Constitution of the Reformed Dutch Church of North America, 1833, Chapter I, Article I.4.sec. 2, in Corwin, *Digest*, xi.
[12] Constitution, 1833, Chapter I, Article I.4.sec. 2.
[13] Corwin, *Digest*, 215.

that in the current practice of the church, the historical remnant of dispensations can be found in both the Ministerial Formation Certification Agency and in the Approved Alternate Route. While it is difficult to determine the exact nature of all the dispensations given, the spirit remains the same. There are particular circumstances when certain requirements may be waived by the General Synod for a variety of reasons.

In 1877, the General Synod declared the classes the custodians of applications for dispensations, because the classes were the most familiar with the candidates and the particular circumstances surrounding the applications.[14] Applications, then, were still approved by the General Synod, but they were handled through the classes.

Although often discouraged, dispensations were not an uncommon occurrence. Several times the General Synod sought to encourage the church to be discerning in their requests for dispensations In 1891, in response to many applications for dispensations by the classes, "the General Synod do[es] hereby enjoin the various Classes to observe great caution in reference to these applications, to scrutinize carefully and to discriminate wisely."[15] Furthermore, in 1895, the General Synod noted that in light of the number of dispensations for the educational requirements for the ministry, "(1) The Reformed Church in America should continue to maintain the historic high standard of literary attainments in its ministry. (2) To this end recommendations for the exercise of the dispensing power should be made by Classes only when circumstances the most extraordinary imperatively demand it."[16] Further, in 1900 the synod declared, "The Synod reaffirms the principle that dispensations shall not be granted except under unusual circumstances."[17]

A review of Mildred Schuppert's *Digest and Index of the Minutes of the General Synod of the Reformed Church in America*[18] shows a number of actions of the General Synod regarding dispensations from the professorial certificate, as well as the express desire for Reformed Church

---

[14] Corwin, *Digest,* 215.
[15] Corwin, *Digest,* 215.
[16] Corwin, *Digest,* 215.
[17] Corwin, *Digest,* 217.
[18] Mildred Schuppert, *Digest and Index of the Minutes of the General Synod of the Reformed Church in America, 1958-1977,* The Historical Series of the Reformed Church in America 7 (Grand Rapids, MI: Eerdmans, 1979); Schuppert, *Digest and Index 1906-1957,* The Historical Series of the Reformed Church in America 8 (Grand Rapids, MI: Eerdmans, 1982).

ministers to study at Reformed Church seminaries. It is important to remember, though, that dispensations could only be granted by the General Synod, not by a classis or theological school.[19]

In 1994, the General Synod voted to appoint a Task Force on Standards for the Preparation for the Professional Ministry in the Reformed Church in America[20] to "determine whether the process leading to ordination provides the Reformed Church in America with the quality and quantity of ministerial leadership it requires."[21] In 1997, the task force submitted its report to the General Synod.[22] In the report, the task force identified an "Approved Alternate Route" because "[i]n certain circumstances, candidates may qualify for ordination in the RCA through an alternate process."[23] The application, then, was to be submitted to the to-be-formed (at the time) Ministerial Formation Coordinating Agency, which would make acceptances or rejections of those applications.[24]

In 1998, the General Synod voted to remove the section on dispensations, and add a section in the *BCO* about an "approved alternate route."[25]

Commissioned Preaching Elders

The problem of an insufficient membership to support a full-time minister is by no means a new problem, but as we saw above, was a problem with which even the Dutch colonies struggled. Similarly, this is not a problem that disappeared but has often remained with us. In 1981, in response to an overture by the Classis of Montgomery, the General Synod voted to instruct the Commission on Church Order (CCO) to study the "status and function of stated supply ministers and the potential for lay ministers."[26]

In 1982, the CCO responded that there was no presence of "lay ministers" in the BCO, and determined that a study of them would need to be conducted. In 1982, the General Synod Executive Council approved the formation of the Committee on Plurality and Flexibility

---

[19] William Demarest, *Notes on the Constitution of the Reformed Church in America,* rev. ed. (New Brunswick, NJ: New Brunswick Theological Seminary, 1946).
[20] *MGS* 1994, 278.
[21] *MGS* 1994, 278.
[22] *MGS* 1997, 330–52.
[23] *MGS* 1997, 346.
[24] *MGS* 1997, 346.
[25] *MGS* 1998, 368–74.
[26] *MGS* 1981, 211.

of the Ministry.[27] In 1984, this committee recommended to the General Synod, among other things, to create the designation of "licensed elder," which would entail preaching and administration of the sacraments, allow for the solemnization of marriages if allowed by state law, and represent the congregation at classis meetings. This recommendation was not adopted. Among the concerns were that it would remove the need for congregations to call ministers, it would bypass the supervision of theological education by the Board of Theological Education, it would weaken the Reformed emphasis of an educated clergy and "would make the present over-supply of ministers even worse."[28]

This possibility, however, was not realized. In 1988, the report of the Committee on Ecclesiastical Office and Ministry addressed, again, the possibility that people who are not ordained as ministers could fill the pulpit during a vacancy or serve a small church not able to afford a full-time pastor. Further, the committee noted, "the RCA may also want to consider opening the ordained ministry of the Word to gifted elders who have proven their effectiveness in the area of pastoral leadership for an appropriate period of time."[29]

In response to another overture, in 1994, the General Synod voted to instruct the CCO to "study the feasibility of setting up a process to certify qualified laity for ministry."[30] The next year, the CCO recommended the inclusion of "licensed lay minister" in the BCO, and the General Synod referred this matter to the Commission on Theology (COT) for study.[31]

In 1996, the COT submitted a paper entitled "The Commissioning of Preaching Elders," and the General Synod voted to distribute it to RCA congregations for study, comment, and response to the COT.[32] In 1997, the COT, after incorporating feedback, resubmitted the paper to the General Synod, as well as changes to the Book of Church Order for implementation.[33]

The paper sought to balance the needs of the church with the distinctions among the ministries of the offices of elder and minister. The COT acknowledged the reality that many small-membership churches cannot afford a full-time minister and that there may be

[27] *MGS* 1982, 172.
[28] *MGS* 1984, 182.
[29] MGS 1988, 135.
[30] *MGS* 1994, 249.
[31] *MGS* 1995, 217.
[32] *MGS* 1996, 398.
[33] *MGS* 1997, 283–85.

others with gifts for preaching, as well as the fact that the office of minister "is not alone in its responsibility to guide and direct the whole church in its proclamation of the gospel."[34] Indeed, this responsibility is shared with elders.

In recommending the commissioning of preaching elders, the commission did acknowledge that "[i]f elders are to preach, it must be recognized that this distinction of roles would become somewhat blurred. The commission does not believe that such blurring distorts the function of the offices unduly if other safeguards are in place."[35] In fact, this may help to emphasize the fact that the offices of minister and elder are not completely different, but differ in kind, that is, a minister is an elder of a special order.[36]

Elders serve with the ministers but are not identical. Elders oversee the preaching of the Word while ministers are the ones who carry that out that preaching; elders "[do] not forsake a worldly calling"[37] as ministers do, and the office and role of "elder is bound more closely to a local congregation than the authority of a minister of Word and sacrament."[38] In its paper, the COT noted that this distinction is worth upholding, even as elders may engage in the preaching of the Word. Therefore, preaching elders were not to be free to preach within any church in the classis or any church in the denomination, but were to be authorized to preach in a "particular congregation" so as not to lose the role of the office of elder.[39]

Furthermore, the paper stated that

> [A]ny authorization of an elder to preach should not imply authority to exercise any other pastoral or official functions beyond those normally exercised by elders. The authorization of preaching elders does not confer the authority to perform marriages, preside over consistories, preside over congregational meetings, use the title "pastor," engage in pastoral counseling (unless appropriately trained for this function as an elder), or claim ministerial status for tax purposes. The authorization of an elder to preach should convey authority to fulfill the normal

---

[34] *MGS* 1997, 278.
[35] *MGS* 1997, 280.
[36] *MGS* 1997, 280.
[37] *MGS* 1997, 280.
[38] *MGS* 1997, 281.
[39] *MGS* 1997, 281.

functions of an elder and to preach in a local congregation. That is all.[40]

Therefore, in its paper, the COT sought to uphold the uniqueness and nuances of the offices while at the same time allowing for the provision of the preaching of the Word in churches that may not have the ability to support a minister of Word and sacrament.

Commissioned Pastors

Just a few short years after the inclusion of commissioned preaching elders in the *BCO*, the president of the 2001 General Synod proposed to convene a one-time summit to:

> study the concept of lay pastoral ministry in the RCA, in order to meet the need for pastoral leadership in churches unable to afford or attract full-time ministers of Word and sacrament and to equip gifted lay leadership being called by God into the mission of the church.[41]

The General Synod approved the convening of this summit, with a report back to the General Synod of 2002.[42]

At the time, there was concern in the RCA regarding a shortage of ministers of Word and sacrament, as well as a concern that there would not be enough leaders for the number of 201 churches that were envisioned to be planted,[43] especially in the Regional Synod of the Far West.[44] Some estimates predicted that the RCA would need upward of four hundred new pastors within five years. To meet this need, there was discussion at this time to expand the preaching elder to serve in much the same way as ministers.[45] However, this estimation of a significant shortage of ministers was not universally accepted. Indeed, others argued that there were ministers and candidates for ministry without calls.[46] In fact, it has been demonstrated that concerns about

---

[40] *MGS* 1997, 281.
[41] *MGS* 2001, 37–38.
[42] *MGS* 2001, 275.
[43] Wesley Granberg-Michaelson, "Leaders Needed," *The Church Herald*, March 2001, 12.
[44] Shannon Bolkema, "Regional Synods Seek 'Ordained Evangelists,'" *The Church Herald*, September 2001, 10.
[45] Gene Vander Well, "Unleashing the Laity," *The Church Herald*, September 2000, 30.
[46] Eric Titus, "'No' to Commissioned Pastors," *The Church Herald*, February 2004, 6; Corstian DeVos, "Flak and Flattery," *The Church Herald*, April 2004, 4–5.

a shortage of ministers is not new, and the RCA has dealt with cycles of shortage and surplus of ministerial supply in the first half of the twentieth century and the church had adapted to these and maintained educational standards for ministers.[47]

In 2002, the participants of the summit reported back to the General Synod. In the report, the summit participants identified four leadership-related problems to be addressed:

1. Many pastoral openings in various congregational settings are not being filled by our current supply of ordained ministers of Word and sacrament because of the location of the opening, the financial limitations of the churches, or a lack of interested candidates.
2. There is a shortage of trained ministers of Word and sacrament to expand the RCA's ministry to include more church starts, enhanced youth ministry, new staff positions, and emerging fields of ministry.
3. People who are raised up by their congregations (for example, racial/ethnic, rural, and small-membership churches) and are clearly called by God to lead their church are sometimes unable to complete in-residence theological training due to family obligations, finances, age, or the need to stay in an already-established ministry.
4. Some potential leaders in our midst—gifted, dedicated, knowledgeable laity within the RCA who are called by God to serve—have no clear, attainable pathway to receive training nor a clearly defined position within the denomination to reach for.[48]

The participants of the summit determined that these four problems could be addressed by the creation of a designation of "'commissioned pastor,' which would require an intermediate level of professional theological training available close to home, and provide the credentials to serve within the bounds of a classis."[49] The General Synod voted to adopt this new ministry designation.[50]

Unlike the commissioned preaching elder, the role of the commissioned pastor was designed to be broader, and included other

---

[47] George Brown Jr., "Ministerial Supply, 1900-1950: A Historical Perspective," unpublished paper, 2003.
[48] *MGS* 2002, 292.
[49] *MGS* 2002, 292.
[50] *MGS* 2002, 293.

pastoral tasks such as serving as the presiding officer of a consistory under the supervision of a classical supervisor, performing marriages when allowed by state law, presiding at the ordination and installation of elders and deacons, and administering the sacraments.[51] The report acknowledged the (relatively new at the time) role of preaching elder, but also noted that this designation "[does] not offer the degree of flexibility and authority that comes with this new designation of commissioned pastor."[52]

Because of the recent adoption of this designation, the commission was able to talk with several people who were a part of the Lay Pastoral Ministry Summit to gain additional insight into the origin of this ministry designation. Originally, the designation of commissioned pastor was intended to be for people who were already involved in and effective in ministry, providing more resourcing and commissioning to their ministry work. Due to this, the commissioned pastor designation was not intended to be an entry point into ministry, but was intended to enhance and resource people who were already in ministry, with the goal of helping these people to eventually enter seminary and work toward the possibility of the ministry of Word and sacrament. The original intention was that commissioned pastors would serve alongside, and under supervision of, ministers of Word and sacrament, and they were never intended to replace or serve as a substitute for a minister (or serve on their own). It was also never envisioned that commissioned pastors would be delegates to the General Synod. Unlike ministers, whose training and education is overseen by the General Synod, the training for commissioned pastors was delegated to the classes, and therefore commissioned pastors could not move between classes, as ministers may.[53]

Throughout their report, the commissioned pastor was referred to as a ministry designation to which one is commissioned, and not as an office to which one is ordained or installed. Attached to the creation of a new ministry designation were other recommendations, which included the instruction of the Commission on Church Order (CCO) to propose revisions to the BCO to include commissioned pastors,[54] which was put forth by the CCO in 2003. In particular, it was required that a

[51] *MGS* 2002, 295.
[52] *MGS* 2002, 297.
[53] Glenn DeMaster, personal communication, February 2, 2015; Phyllis Palsma, personal communication, January 29, 2015; Cora Taitt, personal communication, February 2, 2015; Rodney Veldhuizen, personal communication, February 6, 2015.
[54] *MGS* 2002, 297.

candidate who is recommended by a consistory to be a commissioned pastor would already be an elder at the time of recommendation.[55] The minutes record an amendment to the floor allowing for members who are not elders to be recommended and that the individual would then be ordained to the office of elder before proceeding through the training program. Although this amendment was not adopted,[56] it is worth noting because a similar revision will be addressed at a later point.

Two years later, the Classis of West Sioux overtured the General Synod to allow not only an elder to be recommended as commissioned pastor candidate but also "a person with gifts for and a heart set upon the office of elder."[57] In the reasoning for this amendment, it was argued that requiring a potential candidate to be ordained as an elder before being recommended limited the number of candidates able to be considered as commissioned pastors, and that "[t]he current standard severely limits the opportunities for women to be trained as commissioned pastors as the church is still transitioning out of the reality of male-dominated office holders."[58] In response to the overture, General Synod directed the CCO to propose an amendment to the BCO that "implements the intention of [the] overture."[59]

The CCO, in 2006, responded to the instruction and offered an amendment that would allow for consistories to recommend "a confessing member of a Reformed Church" rather than "an elder" to the classis as a candidate for commissioned pastor, which was adopted by the General Synod.[60] In the proposal of this change, however, the CCO did express cautionary notes in its report, which are valuable to this discussion and included here at length.

> [J]ust such "early identification" is itself a problem from the perspective of church order. The commissioned pastor is tied to the notion of office. Office is conferred by ordination, and ordination to the office of elder presumes election by a congregation. For that reason neither a person's gifts nor personal desire by themselves can identify "future elders" (or deacons).
>
> The proposal also raises the specter of persons who intend to be ordained elder in order that he or she may become

---

[55] *MGS* 2003, 209–11.
[56] *MGS* 2003, 209.
[57] *MGS* 2005, 297.
[58] *MGS* 2005, 298.
[59] *MGS* 2005, 298.
[60] *MGS* 2006, 69.

a commissioned pastor. The goal is commissioned pastor; the means to the goal is to be ordained elder. But that, too, is a violation of a Reformed understanding of office, particularly of the office of elder. It devalues that office to that of "second-class." Furthermore, it imports an episcopal understanding of office whereby one is ordained to an office "on the way" to a so-called "higher" office.

Some may argue that this makes the route to commissioned pastor more difficult. That difficulty is in fact intended. Commissioned pastors are an exception in the order, and not the rule.[61]

Therefore, the training for commissioned pastors was created to parallel that of ministers, that is, a member of a Reformed church may finish the training program but has no guarantee of ordination to the office of elder and therefore no guarantee to serve as a commissioned pastor, just as with ministers, graduating from seminary is no guarantee to ordination as a minister.[62] A potential negative of this, however, is that it further blurred the distinction between ministers and commissioned pastors, and between office and function.

Commissioned pastors, then, functionally occupy a middle ground of sorts between preaching elders and ministers of Word and sacrament. The commissioned pastor designation was never intended or designed to serve as a replacement for the minister of Word and sacrament, nor was it intended to be an easier path to professional ministry; it was intended to support, and be supervised by, ministers in a specific place within a classis for a specific period of time.

Conclusion

This paper has sought to outline the history of the commissioned pastor designation, and also to place the commissioned pastor in historical context with other ways that the church has endeavored to address the needs of the ministry. Throughout its history, the Reformed Church has sought different ways to meet the needs of ministry in the various situations in which it found itself.

There have been times in which the pool of clergy has waxed and waned. During times in which clergy were more scarce, the Reformed Church has sought ways to ensure two things: first, that the faithful

[61] *MGS* 2006, 69.
[62] *MGS* 2006, 69.

could have a pastoral presence, and second, that the essence of the church and the importance of office is maintained. From comforters of the sick to the process of dispensation, to preaching elders, to commissioned pastors, the RCA has dealt with the needs of the church in several creative ways. However, it has also placed limitations on functions as well, so as to maintain the distinction, uniqueness, nuances, and parity of the offices. The RCA has upheld its emphasis on an educated ministry, even as it has empowered elders, deacons, and members in various ways. As we continue to offer the world a distinctly Reformed witness, it is important that we are intentional about the ways in which we evaluate and adapt to challenges that we experience.

CHAPTER 11

A Brief History of Schism and Separation in the Reformed Church in America Along with a Summary of the Creeds and Confessions as Statements of Unity[1]

The Church's one foundation is Jesus Christ her Lord;
She is his new creation by water and the Word.
From heaven he came and sought her to be his holy bride;
With his own blood he bought her, and for her life he died.[2]

Introduction

    Not everyone decries ecclesiastical discord. For many, living up to the Reformed Church in America's (RCA) motto *Eendracht Maakt Macht* ("Concord Makes Strength") comes at too great a price.[3] In *Loyalty and Loss: The Reformed Church in America, 1945-1994*, Lynn Japinga makes a distinction that "the most divisive conflicts in the Reformed Church

---

[1] *Minutes of General Synod* (hereafter *MGS*) 2016, 278–90.
[2] Samuel J. Stone, "The Church's One Foundation," in *Rejoice in the Lord: A Hymn Companion to the Scriptures*, ed. Erik Routley (Grand Rapids, MI: Eerdmans, 1985), #394.
[3] The RCA acronym will be used throughout to identify the Reformed Church in America, even when referring to points in history when the denomination was known as the Reformed Protestant Dutch Church.

did not arise between fundamentalists and modernists, because the denomination had very few modernists."[4] While acknowledging the "limits of labels," Japinga posits three distinctive partisan groups within the denomination that form a useful model for comprehending the process and outcomes of the RCA's polemics.

On one side there are the "purists" that consider themselves "truly reformed," though their theology tends to be shaped more by American fundamentalist views of the Bible and church than by Reformed tradition.[5] On the other side of the aisle are the "moderates." Japinga identifies the moderates as:

> ...profoundly shaped by Reformed theology, polity, and liturgy. They valued the Bible but were not literalist in their reading of it. They were ecumenical, because they believed that God had not entrusted the whole of the gospel to the Reformed Church in America. They trusted that God brought the church into being and that God would protect it, so Christians did not need to be so anxious about its purity.[6]

Lying between these poles are the "conservatives," those who were theologically conservative but tended toward ecumenism and could therefore live with the ambiguity of less than full agreement. It is necessary to keep in mind that each of these nomenclatures encapsulates a complex belief system, full of nuance and rife with exceptions. For instance, to assume that any particular geographical area is the locus of one party or the other falls very short of realizing the richness of our history. For our congregations in all areas wrestled with, and continue to wrestle with, issues that set neighboring churches apart and have even divided congregations.

It is instructive to consider James W. Van Hoeven's opening words in his preface to *Word and World: Reformed Theology in America*:

> Christian theology exists in the context of history. This means that Christian theology is necessarily dynamic and developing, is shaped in each new age by the interaction of the biblical Word with the contemporary world...Thus no church, properly

---

[4] See Lynn Japinga, *Loyalty and Loss: The Reformed Church in America, 1945-1994*, The Historical Series of the Reformed Church in America 77 (Grand Rapids, MI: Eerdmans, 2013), 18.
[5] Japinga, *Loyalty and Loss*, 18.
[6] Japinga, *Loyalty and Loss*, 19.

speaking, can claim that its theology is original; in every period Christian theology is in some sense "mottled."⁷

Perhaps, then, we should be advised that ecclesiastical discord is no more or less the growing pains of a church Transformed and Transforming, but a necessary dialogue for a church with a history and a future.

The following paper will summarize three rancorous events of schism within, and in two cases secession from, the RCA. The first is the Coetus and Conferentie schism that raged for more than 15 years. Even after the Plan of Union was signed in 1771, the hostilities continued incarnate in the Tory and Rebel alliances during the American Revolution. Moreover, after the war and subsequent constitution of a new American denomination, a group from the Hackensack Valley of New Jersey seceded in 1822 under the self-imposed moniker of the "True Dutch Reformed Church." This somewhat bizarre chapter in church history will be the subject of the second event discussed. The third event will be the schism (with theological roots in the Hackensack Valley secession) that emboldened a handful of individuals from Grand Rapids, Michigan, to withdraw from the RCA in 1856 to form the Christian Reformed Church. The exodus from the RCA intensified in 1882 over the issue of freemasonry and continued to assert a deleterious effect on church growth, as new immigrants eschewed the RCA to join the decidedly less-Americanized Christian Reformed Church. A brief discussion of the nature and contexts of three unity statements, the Heidelberg Catechism, the Belgic Confession, and the Belhar Confession, will conclude this paper. Finally, five verses of the hymn "The Church's One Foundation" are interposed between subject headings for the reader's reflection.

Competing Theologies

In the 1730s, a controversy arose in the Dutch Reformed Church in the American colonies when a movement known as the Great Awakening swept through the mid-Atlantic on the wings of men like Dutch Reformed itinerant preacher Theodorus Jacobus Frelinghuysen (1691-1747).[8] Since the arrival of the Dutch in Manhattan in the 1620s,

---

[7] See James W. Van Hoeven, ed., *Word and World: Reformed Theology in America*, The Historical Series of the Reformed Church in America 16 (Grand Rapids, MI: Eerdmans. 1986), xi.

[8] The pietistic revivalism preaching of Frelinghuysen and a group of itinerant preachers such as James Davenport (1716–57), Jonathan Edwards (1703–58), Gilbert Tennent

nothing in more than 100 years had rocked the pristine Synod of Dort's orthodox theology. Indeed, its practice so geographically distant from the mother church had endowed it with a particular status and exigency. Not even the conquest of the British in 1664, though having a deep and lasting impact on the Dutch Reformed Church institution, could diminish the church's entrenched Calvinism. Nevertheless, the theological roots of this controversy can be traced to the rivalry between strict Calvinists and the Arminians during the Synod of Dort in 1618-19. As Donald J. Bruggink and Kim N. Baker summarized in *By Grace Alone: Stories of the Reformed Church in America*, opposing groups, called conventicles, were formed, with the Arminian side emphasizing the "personal religious experience" of its members and the strict Calvinist side stressing the "rational examination of scripture and its meaning."[9]

John W. Beardslee's chapter in *Word and World* summarizes the post-Frelinghuysen shift in theology as follows:

> One of the basic theological problems that surfaced after Frelinghuysen's arrival, and which has troubled the Dutch church from that day forward, concerned the nature of the Christian church. Because the formal definition of the church was not in dispute, this problem churned beneath the surface. It is best reflected in a popular eighteenth century textbook on dogmatics written by Johannes á Marck, and taught to future clergy of the Reformed Church at New Brunswick Seminary. In his dogmatics, Marck lists the marks of the church, those visible signs by which the true church could be recognized in the world. He recognized at least five marks: the classical three of Reformed theology (pure preaching, legitimate administration of the sacraments, and Christian discipline), plus holiness of life and fraternal love. Marck gives as his preference a two-fold structure: purity of doctrine as "a priori" and "antecedent," and holiness of life as "a posteriori" and "consequent." The shift in the Reformed Doctrine of the church is obvious in this: The church of the word and sacrament was becoming the church of the word and personal holiness. The influence of pietism on mainstream Reformed orthodoxy was being felt.[10]

(1703–64), and George Whitefield (1714–70) issued a direct challenge to the theological primacy of Calvinism in America.

9   Donald J. Bruggink and Kim Nathan Baker, *By Grace Alone: Stories of the Reformed Church in America*, The Historical Series of the Reformed Church in America 44 (Grand Rapids: Eerdmans, 2013), 121.

10 John W. Beardslee III, "Orthodoxy and Piety: Two Styles of Faith in the Colonial Period," in Van Hoeven, *Word and World*, 10–11.

While it is tempting to say more about the nature and impact of Frelinghuysen's preaching, I am resigned in a short paper to say that regarding the Dutch Reformed Church in America, the die had been cast between those favoring orthodoxy and a close union with the Church in the Netherlands, and those whose unique American brand of piety and evangelistic fervor would fly in the face of that tradition. Later we shall see how the Rev. John Henry Livingston (1746–1825) draws these seemingly diametric tendencies together in a prodigious act of unity.[11]

Elect from every nation, yet one o'er all the earth;
Her charter of salvation, "One Lord, one faith, one birth!"
One holy name she blesses, partakes one holy food,
And to one hope she presses with every grace endued.

The Coetus and Conferentie Schism

A source of consternation among the Dutch clergy in America centered on the slow and cumbersome process of dealing with the distant Classis of Amsterdam. Disputes often took months to settle. Consequently, issues of discipline festered without a local power to intervene. An even greater concern was for the many vacant pulpits that could be supplied only by ministers who were educated, examined, and ordained in the Netherlands. Thus, if a local candidate was found, he would be required to undergo the journey to the Netherlands to prepare and be ordained in ministry, then journey back to be installed. Oceanic travel was long and perilous.[12] Furthermore, that individual would be away for several years, a luxury many believed the church could not afford.

The suggestion to form a fraternal clerical organization in America to instill better communication was made as early as 1662 by

---

[11] For further investigation of the impact of the "Great Awakening" and Theodorus Frelinghuysen on the Dutch Reformed Church, the following books are recommended: Randall H. Balmer, *A Perfect Babel of Confusion: Dutch Religion and English Culture in the Middle Colonies* (New York: Oxford University Press, 1989); Joel R. Beeke, ed., *Forerunner of the Great Awakening: Sermons by Theodorus Jacobus Frelinghuysen (1691- 1747)*, The Historical Series of the Reformed Church in America 36 (Grand Rapids, Michigan: Eerdmans, 2000); and Leon van den Broeke, Hans Krabbendam, and Dirk Mouw, eds., *Transatlantic Pieties: Dutch Clergy in Colonial America,* The Historical Series of the Reformed Church in America 76 (Grand Rapids, MI: Eerdmans, 2013).

[12] Bruggink and Baker, *By Grace Alone*, 54. Theodore Frelinghuysen, the son of the famous Raritan itinerant preacher, was captured at sea and detained six months after attending a Dutch ordination. Two of his brothers were drowned at sea while returning to America from their own ordinations.

Domine Johannes T. Polhemus (1598-1676) of Flatbush, New York. In 1706 Gualterus Dubois (1666-1751), Vincentius Anthonides (1670-1744), and Henricus Beys (born c. 1680) made a formal request to the Classis of Amsterdam to allow Dutch clergy in colonial America to hold a formal gathering once a year. In 1709 the Classis of Amsterdam summarily denied the request by saying that "the formation of a classis among you, to correspond to ours at home, is yet far in the future."[13]

Yet, after a protracted period of correspondence over the Frelinghuysen disputes, the Classis of Amsterdam lifted its injunction. In 1738, the first meeting of the fraternal organization of clergy in America known as a Coetus took place with 10 of the 14 Dutch ministers residing in colonial New Jersey and New York in attendance.[14] Although the measure did nothing to abrogate the authority of the Classis of Amsterdam over the Dutch clergy in the New World, the four ministers who had absented themselves from the first meeting did so because they feared the members of the Coetus had designs on forming an independent classis. In their estimation, such a measure may be interpreted by the British Crown as a violation of the Charter of 1696 granting the Dutch Church ecclesiastical liberty in colonial America as long as it remained under the control of the Classis of Amsterdam. The four dissenting ministers became representatives of an opposing group called the Conferentie, who shared a concern for preserving the high standards of education and orthodoxy among the ministry and for leaving judicial matters in the hands of the Classis of Amsterdam.[15]

The members of the Conferentie were correct that the Coetus would put forth a plan to become an independent classis. That action came in 1754 and incited a bitter dispute lasting 15 years.[16] By the 1760s division between the opposing Coetus and Conferentie parties had reached a state of crisis in which the rancor resulted in hostilities between neighboring churches and even dividing some congregations. Arie Brouwer makes this colorful summary:

---

[13] Bruggink and Baker, *By Grace Alone*, 51.

[14] The articles of incorporation can be found in Edward Tanjore Corwin, *A Digest of Constitutional and Synodical Legislation of the Reformed Church in America* (New York: Board of Publication of the Reformed Church in America, 1906), 147–49. The minutes of this body from 1755 to 1771 are reprinted in Volume V of Hugh Hastings, ed., *Ecclesiastical Records of the State of New York* (Albany, NY: James B. Lyon, State Printer, 1901). It is in itself a comment on how slow communications came from the Classis of Amsterdam that the final approval for forming the Coetus wasn't received until 1747, nine years after the request had been made.

[15] By 1765, the Conferentie had ten members but was still a minority.

[16] See Corwin, *Digest*, 141–42, for the articles of incorporation as a separate classis.

The controversy was fierce. Both sides published pamphlets filled with acrimonious personal attacks. As the dispute became public knowledge, allegiance to the Classis of Amsterdam was sometimes seen as disloyalty to the British crown. Neighboring ministers spurned one another; congregations divided, some alternating Sundays in the same sanctuary and others locking the doors against the opposing side. When some of the Coetus party met at Poughkeepsie for an ordination, the Conferentie group seized the church building and barred the door. The ordination proceeded under a large tree in the church yard. In other places, particularly in the Hackensack Valley, even husbands and wives, parents and children sometimes opposed each other.[17]

Archibald Laidlie (1727-79), a Dutch Reformed minister in New York who was the first to preach in English and a member of the Coetus party, convinced John Henry Livingston (1746-1825) to help bring peace to the fractured Dutch Reformed Church. A native-born American, Livingston learned the Dutch language and traveled to Utrecht, Holland, to receive his theological education and ordination. During this time he met with the Classis of Amsterdam to apprise them of the situation and to lay out a plan of resolution. In 1768 he submitted a plan of union to the colonies.[18] Although his first plan failed to gain support, his second plan containing 35 articles was approved by a quorum of 22 Coetus and Conferentie American clergymen in 1771 and ratified by the Classis of Amsterdam in 1772.[19] The plan permitted the American church to educate and ordain its own ministers, satisfying the Coetus. Likewise, the plan appeased the Conferentie by having

---

[17] Arie R. Brouwer, *Reformed Church Roots: Thirty-Five Formative Events* (New York: Reformed Church Press, 1977), 62.

[18] The plan proposed a professorship of theology at Princeton, a measure likely influenced by Livingston's contact in Utrecht with Princeton president-elect John Witherspoon (1723–94). Opposing the professorship at Princeton was Domine Johannes Ritzema (1710–88), who had served as Coetus secretary but seceded to the Conferentie because he had wanted to establish the theology professorship at King's College (now Columbia University). It appears Ritzema had self interest in this design by inveigling friends to supply his name as the intended theology professor at King's College. Ritzema's plot was unveiled and became a source of personal embarrassment. An account of Ritzema's role in the Coetus/Conferentie schism can be found in Edward Tanjore Corwin, *Manual of the Reformed Church in America*, 4th ed. (New York: Board of Publication of the Reformed Church in America, 1902), in the "History" section and the "Ministry" component under Ritzema's name.

[19] John Henry Livingston presided over the peace convention that took place in New York City. See Corwin, *Digest*, 142.

retained the authority of the Classis of Amsterdam and the Synod of North Holland to review all decisions made in America and to appoint the American professor of theology.[20]

The Coetus had secured a charter for Queens College (now Rutgers) in 1770 to be a school for training the ministry of the Dutch churches in America. In 1773 at the Convention in Kingston, it was resolved to ask the Classis of Amsterdam to send a professor of theology from Holland. The classis consulted with the theological faculty at Utrecht and agreed to recommend Livingston instead. He would have been appointed in 1775, but the war broke out. In 1784, Livingston was unanimously elected seminary professor, marking the beginning of New Brunswick Theological Seminary.[21]

Arie Brouwer summarizes, "On the whole, the Coetus sought to expand the church through renewal and evangelism; the Conferentie sought to preserve the church by conserving the tradition."[22]

Though with a scornful wonder, we see her sore oppressed,
By schisms rent asunder, by heresies distressed,
Yet saints their watch are keeping, their cry goes up, "How long?"
And soon the night of weeping shall be the morn of song!

The True Dutch Reformed Church (TDRC) Secession of 1822

The early days of a new country and a new denomination didn't necessarily bring harmony to every hamlet. The dividing lines of the Coetus and Conferentie schism, though nominally settled with Livingston's plan of union in 1771, continued to be played out in terms of Tory and Rebel sympathies during the American Revolution.[23] After

---

[20] Categorically the plan called for: a) the internal arrangement and government of the churches and the organization of superior church judicatories for the establishment of a professorship for the education of ministers, and for the founding of schools; b) the healing of dissensions in the various churches; and c) correspondence with the Church in Holland. It was provided that the minutes of the ecclesiastical courts be sent to the Classis of Amsterdam, and that the classis, or if need be, the Synod of Holland, might be appealed to in cases of difficulty.

[21] John Coakley, *New Brunswick Theological Seminary: An Illustrated History, 1784–2014*, The Historical Series of the Reformed Church in America 83 (Grand Rapids, MI: Eerdmans, 2014), 2–3.

[22] Brouwer, *Reformed Church Roots*, 62.

[23] See Beardslee, "Orthodoxy and Piety." The members of the Coetus, who had brought about an independent classis and who were ultimately the framers of the new Reformed Church in America's constitution, were most likely to support the cause for freedom from British rule. Conversely, those in the Conferentie generally sided with the Tories, as they were largely content with the English rule, the English

the war, concerns over doctrinal purity arose as the newly christened Reformed Protestant Dutch Church in America forged ecumenical ties with other communions as per the Articles of Correspondence with the Presbyterian and Associate Reformed Churches in 1785. With incorporation came a new constitution assigning classes that enjoined, in some cases, neighboring churches that had been on opposing sides during the war. Even a new English language hymnal compiled for the denomination by John Henry Livingston caused a furor, as many speculated their new American denomination had become too American.[24] According to Arie Brower:

> The lingering animosity resulting from the controversies may well have been the decisive factor which kept the Reformed Church from realizing the potential of the great American expansion that followed the Revolutionary War. The church could not organize to act. Vital energies were consumed with petitions, complaints and quarrels. Livingston himself was able to fuse the theology and piety of a tradition with a passion for the unity and expansion of the church. The church he served could not.[25]

Such was the case in the two neighboring Bergen County, New Jersey, churches of Hackensack and Schraalenbergh, who were at one time united under the care of Antonius Curtenius.[26] In 1748, Johannes Henricus Goetschius was called to be a colleague of the aging Curtenius. While both ministers were at that time members of the Coetus, Curtenius and several followers became ardent objectors to the party

---

Charter of 1696, and continued to recognize the Netherlands as their spiritual home and ecclesiastical authority. Donald Bruggink and Kim Baker point out in *By Grace Alone* that, of 41 Dutch Reformed ministers who were active at the time of the American Revolution, eight were either Tory or sympathetic to the British cause.

[24] For an excellent treatment of the impacts felt and alliances made by the Constitution of the Reformed Dutch Reformed Church in the United States of America, see Daniel J. Meeter, *Meeting Each Other in Doctrine, Liturgy, and Government*, The Historical Series of the Reformed Church in America 24 (Grand Rapids, MI: Eerdmans, 1993).

[25] Brouwer, *Reformed Church Roots*, 64.

[26] See Corwin, *Manual*, under "The Ministry" entries for Antonius Curtenius (1698–1756), Johannes Henricus Goetschius (1718–74), Solomon Froeligh (1750–1827), and Warmoldus Kuypers (1732–97). See also "History of the Churches of Hackensack and Schraalenbergh," in Benjamin Cook Taylor, *Annals of the Classis of Bergen, of the Reformed Dutch Church, and of the Churches Under Its Care, Including the Civil History of the Ancient Township of Bergen in New Jersey*, 3rd ed. (New York: Board of Publication of the Reformed Protestant Dutch Church, 1857) 170–248; Jacob Brinkerhoff, *The History of the True Dutch Reformed Church in the United States of America* (New York: E. B. Tripp, 1873).

when the Coetus proposed becoming a classis in 1753. Party lines were drawn between Curtenius and Goetschius factions, signified by the two churches forming separate consistories.[27]

For Solomon Froeligh, the time seemed right to quell the animosities between the two churches when he was called to Hackensack in 1786. Warmoldus Kuypers, pastor at Schraalenbergh, was receptive to Froeligh's overtures for reconciliation, and indeed the churches cooperated long enough to build a union church in 1790-95. Some thought it divine providence when in 1795 the union church was struck by lightning, causing the stone above the church door reading *Een dracht Maakt Macht* ("Union Makes Strength") to be broken in two.

The hostilities resurfaced from the consistory at Schraalenbergh after the death of Kuypers (1797), causing Froeligh to surrender his hope of union.[28] As president of the two consistories (one corporation), he cast the deciding vote in an ensuing circus of motions blocking consistory members at Schraalenbergh from attending classis meetings, and more egregiously, that delayed the appointment of Jacobus Van Campen Romeyn (1765-1840) to fill the pulpit at Schraalenbergh. The regional synod stepped in to confirm the appointment of Romeyn and in 1800 placed the churches in separate classes.[29]

In spite of the synod's action to separate the churches by classis, the singular corporation of the two church consistories ensured a feud that lasted for the next 22 years. The two churches vied over properties held in common and fought over where and when to build new churches and parsonages for a growing constituency. Classis intervention was commonplace in the years leading up to 1818, when Froeligh was required to appear before the Classis of Paramus for permitting members to irregularly pass from the Schraalenbergh church to his, and for baptizing the children of the disaffected members.[30]

---

[27] The two consistories were still one corporation. By and large, the consistory of Hackensack aligned with the Coetus and the consistory of Schraalenbergh with the Conferentie. An era of dissention and untoward competition ensued as votes were cast strictly along party lines.

[28] Froeligh's sentiments turned sour, evidenced by his once preaching on the text of Jeremiah 15:19-21, equating his congregation at Hackensack with "the precious" and those at Schraalenbergh with "the vile."

[29] The Classis of Hackensack was dissolved and the Classes of Paramus and Bergen were formed in its place. The synod placed Hackensack under the care of the Classis of Paramus and Schraalenbergh with the Classis of Bergen.

[30] See Taylor, *Annals*. A lengthy series of actions and appeals between the two classes was subsequently elevated to the particular synod resulting in a stalemate on Froeligh's alleged "unconstitutional" behavior. Froeligh's deferral to his consistory as the ruling

In 1822, Solomon Froeligh seceded from the church along with five other ministers to form the True Dutch Reformed Church (TDRC).[31] The group charged that the RCA had become Hopkinsian[32] and thus had surrendered its true Calvinistic roots. Theological differences aside, Froeligh's exit was most likely the result of the pressures he brought to bear in his contumacy, and the subsequent classical deliberations and sanctions he endured. Corwin has even suggested that contributing to Froeligh's departure may have been his disappointment over having not been elected president of New Brunswick Theological Seminary.[33] John Beardslee makes a broader stroke when he posits that the descendants of the Coetus-Whig party in Northern New Jersey had long sought to get out of the denomination.[34] Having been appointed by the General Synod as an assistant professor of theology in 1792, Froeligh was answerable to the General Synod in matters of discipline. He was tried in absentia in 1822 after his departure from the denomination and was subsequently suspended from his professorship and from the ministry.

The 40 or so years of organization under the TDRC banner attracted few new adherents in the eastern U.S.[35] Furthermore, some of the ministers who had united with the TDRC eventually reunited with the RCA. Dr. Froehligh did not return to the RCA and thus remained the TDRC's spiritual head until his death in 1827. The secessionist

body who approved the new members and baptisms certainly muddied the waters of the case against him and raised important questions about the nature and reach of consistorial power.

[31] The other ministers who seceded from the RCA were Abram Brokaw (1793–1846), Sylvanus Palmer (1770–1846), John C. Toll (1799–1848), Henry V. Wyckoff (1771–1835), and Cornelius Demarest (1804-62). Demarest, a former student of Froeligh and pastor of the English Neighborhood Church, was suspended for tampering with the minutes of the Classis of Bergen over the Froeligh affair. Demarest was surely Froeligh's biggest advocate, as can be gleaned from the apologetic text he authored titled Lamentations over Froeligh.

[32] A modified form of Calvinism put forth during the Second Great Awakening by Samuel Hopkins (1721–1803), also known as New Divinity or Edwardseanism (after Jonathan Edwards, 1703–58). The position is known as three-and-a-half-point Calvinism because it denies original sin and teaches that depravity is less than total. Instead, Hopkins stressed a concept founded in humanism known as "disinterested benevolence," in which one denies self-interest or religious aim to perform charitable acts as a social mandate. This notion became an essential building block of the Social Gospel movement in the nineteenth century.

[33] Corwin, Manual, 276. John Henry Livingston was unanimously elected president in 1810.

[34] Beardslee, "Orthodoxy and Piety," 24.

[35] The TDRC had a greater influence on the church in the Midwest and was a factor in the Graafschap and Polkton secession highlighted in the next part of this paper.

church published a magazine called *The Banner of Truth*, which served both as an organ for attacks on the RCA and as a vehicle to spread the TDRC's theological vanguard.[36] In the 1860s the TDRC began an official correspondence with the "True Holland Reformed Church." A union was effected in 1877 and a full merger in 1890 under the newly chosen name of Christian Reformed Church (CRC).[37]

'Mid toil and tribulation, and tumult of her war,
She waits the consummation of peace forevermore,
Till with the vision glorious her longing eyes are blest,
And the great Church victorious shall be the Church at rest.

The Secession of 1856-57 That Produced the Christian Reformed Church

Shortly after William I became the King of Netherlands in 1815, he reorganized the state church. The reorganization brought with it a prevailing wind of rationality that imposed tolerance even among the teachers of private religious schools.[38] For some, William I committed a grave act of interference when he introduced a new hymnal in place of the traditional psalter and imposed the requirement to sing at least one hymn at every service.[39]

In 1834, Hendrik De Cock (1801-1842) seceded from the state Hervormde Kerk (Reformed Church) after having been suspended for publicly lambasting clergy and government officials. Under the Afscheiding (secession) banner, the protest gained traction in Groningen under De Cock, in Utrecht and Noord Brabant under Hendrik P. Scholte (1806-1868), in Gelderland under Anthony Brummelkamp (1811-1888), in Friesland under Simon Van Velzen (1809-1896), in Noord Brabant under Georg Gezelle Meerburg (1806-1855) and in Overijssel

---

[36] Volume IV of *The Banner of Truth* is available on Google Books. See also *True Dutch Reformed Church Acts and Proceedings, Oct 1822–June 1865* (New York: John A. Gray, 1865).

[37] See Janet Sjaarda Sheeres, *Minutes of the Christian Reformed Church*, The Historical Series of the Reformed Church in America 82 (Grand Rapids, MI: Eerdmans, 2014). The former TDRC churches in New Jersey were assigned to the Classis of Hackensack of the Christian Reformed Church.

[38] See Karel Blei, *The Netherlands Reformed Church, 1571-2005*, trans. Allan J. Janssen, The Historical Sries of the Reformed Church in America 51 (Grand Rapids, MI: Eerdmans, 2006).

[39] David M. Tripold, *Sing to the Lord a New Song: Choirs in the Worship and Culture of the Dutch Reformed Church in America, 1785-1860*, The Historical Series of the Reformed Church in America 74 (Grand Rapids, Michigan: Eerdmans, 2012), 23.

under Albertus C. Van Raalte (1811-1876).[40] Thus the bedrock was laid for what Donald J. Bruggink and Kim N. Baker call an "irascible spirit" that arrived in a great Dutch immigration to the American Midwest in the mid-19th century.[41]

This irascible spirit caused Hendrik P. Scholte to form a separatist religious colony in Pella, Iowa.[42] However, Albertus C. Van Raalte, after having founded the Holland, Michigan, colony in 1847, readily united with the RCA in 1850. In *Family Quarrels in the Dutch Reformed Churches of the 19th Century*, Elton Bruins and Robert Swierenga trace a pattern of dissention that led to the 1857 exodus of about ten percent of those who had associated with the RCA.

The controversy stems from the diametric mindsets they herein encapsulate: "The Dutch immigrants from the outset were of two minds, one separatist and oriented to the Christian Seceded Church in the homeland, and the other ecumenical and desirous of reaching out to fellow Reformed believers in the new homeland."[43]

Accusations of heretical teachings were made by some, with Van Raalte himself being the target of slanders regarding his embrace of the American denomination. Others, recalling the hymnal imposed by William I, resented the 800-page compendium of English hymns published by the RCA. On the whole, one can attribute the schism to the Bruins and Swierenga "two minds" summary that equates the particular indoctrinations of those in the Homeland (by geography and association) with a desire to be either a separatist Dutch community in a strange land or to become an integral part of the American fabric.

The schism reached a climax under the leadership of Gijsbert Haan (1801-1874). Haan arrived at the Holland, Michigan, colony in 1849 after having spent time in the East observing the conditions in New York City, in Troy, and at the home of the Western church benefactor and pastor of the Second Reformed Church of Albany, Isaac N. Wyckoff (1792-1869). In Holland and in surrounding communities he spread

---

[40] See Elton J. Bruins and Robert P. Swierenga, *Family Quarrels in the Dutch Reformed Churches in the 19th Century: The Pillar Church Sesquicentennial Lectures*, The Historical Series of the Reformed Church in America 32 (Grand Rapids, MI: Eerdmans, 1999), 22–23. A very accessible summary of Van Raalte's life and work can be found in Jeanne M. Jacobson, Elton J. Bruins, and Larry J. Wagenaar, *Albertus C. Van Raalte: Dutch Leader and American Patriot* (Holland, MI: Hope College, 1996).

[41] Bruggink and Baker, *By Grace Alone*, 118–24.

[42] Eugene P. Heideman, *Hendrik P. Scholte: His Legacy in the Netherlands and in America*, number 84 in *The Historical Series of the Reformed Church in America* (Grand Rapids, MI: Eerdmans, 2015).

[43] Bruins and Swierenga, *Family Quarrels*, 63–64.

the word that the denomination they had joined was "modernistic" (today we use the term liberal), and that he had observed pastors in the East who did not believe in predestination, choirs who disrupted worship with hymn singing, and an elder in Paterson, New Jersey, who did not present his own children for baptism, saying that he wanted them to decide for themselves.[44] In time, Haan became a leading elder and member of the Classis of Grand Rapids. He raised concerns over the RCA's failure to follow the Church Order of Dort and to observe festival days (especially Pentecost). He railed before the General Synod, claiming the Lord's Supper was indiscriminately offered to members of other communions. Moreover, he charged Albertus C. Van Raalte, pastor in Holland, and Cornelius Van Der Meulen (1800-1876), pastor at Zeeland, with disseminating Richard Baxter's (1615-1691) A Call to the Unconverted tract.[45] Citing literature from the 1822 Hackensack secession he had obtained during his stay in the East, Haan voiced a concern over hymn singing and recounted a controversy in Grand Rapids over the election of an elder.[46]

Haan, with a handful of others, seceded from the RCA in October 1856. The following year Hendrik G. Kleijn (1793-1883), Haan's pastor in Grand Rapids, along with the Rev. Koene Van Den Bosch (1818-1897) of Noordeloos (North Holland) and the consistories at Graafschap and Polkton (Coopersville) also exited. The consistory at Graafschap gave the following reasons for uniting with the Separate Reformed Church in the Netherlands:[47]

- The collection of 800 hymns, introduced contrary to church order.
- Inviting [men of] all religious views to the Lord's Supper, excepting Roman Catholics.
- Neglecting to preach the Catechism regularly, [to hold] catechetical classes, and [to do] house visitation.
- That no religious books are circulated without the consent of other denominations, directing your attention to the Sabbath booklet, with the practice by J. Van Der Meulen, in 1855.
- And what grieves our hearts most in all of this is that there are members among you who regard our secession in the Netherlands as not strictly necessary, or [think that] it was untimely.

---

[44] Bruins and Swierenga, *Family Quarrels*, 78.
[45] The tract contains Arminian overtones of universal grace.
[46] Bruins and Swierenga, *Family Quarrels*, 78–80.
[47] Brouwer, *Reformed Church Roots*, 126.

- In the report of Rev. Wyckoff he gives us liberty to walk in this ecclesiastical path.

Albertus C. Van Raalte believed the secession was based on "un-Reformed" principles and offered this scathing comment:

> "Is the fruit of a lust for schism already for a long time manifested by a few leaders, against which there is no weapon, which will do us less damage outside of the church than inside of it. ... Nevertheless, he is constrained with his whole soul to testify against this conduct that tears asunder the church of God, and warns each and every one against such a reckless course of conduct, which will bring ruin upon our posterity. ... the whole affair ... is a mixture of ignorance, sectarianism, and a trampling under foot of the brethren.[48]

The 1857 exodus resulted in about 750 people leaving Holland Classis. In Grand Rapids 100 members joined the new church, in Graafschap 113 members, in Vriesland 15 or 16, and in Noordeloos and Polkton about 20 persons each. Donald J. Bruggink and Kim N. Baker make this observation:[49]

> The real wonder is that the numbers of those who left in 1856-57 were so small (Haan and Kleijn later returned to the Reformed Church). Undoubtedly the leadership of Van Raalte and those of like spirit played a part. For the great majority, the unity of the church (and kindness experienced from the members of the Reformed Church in the East) was more important than the issues.

The Freemason Controversy

By 1880, the fledgling church had only thirty-nine congregations. However, a single issue would have a far-reaching consequence on the ensuing rise in membership of the CRC denomination and, conversely, hinder the growth of the RCA in the Midwest. In 1853, the Classis of Holland condemned Masonic membership as among the "works of darkness" and declared it unlawful for a church member to belong to a Masonic lodge.[50]

---

[48] Brouwer, *Reformed Church Roots*, 126–27.
[49] Bruggink and Baker, *By Grace Alone* 139.
[50] It is helpful to note that Masonic membership in Europe was in effect a rational effrontery to the church. Members were often atheist, deist, or agnostic. Thus, lodge members had largely exchanged religious faith for rational humanism. In the United

Maintaining a European view of Freemasonry, the CRC banned membership in the lodge by synodical order in 1867.[51] The RCA Classis of Wisconsin requested the General Synod follow the lead of the CRC and also ban Masonic membership. However, the General Synod voted to take no action. In 1869 the Classis of Holland joined the Classis of Wisconsin in a new overture that the General Synod assigned to a special committee. In 1870 the General Synod declared that membership in a secret society was "not a good practice" and that church members should not belong. However, the General Synod did not go so far as to ban membership (a thinly-veiled concealment of denominational people in high places who were Masons) and stated further they would not institute a new test for membership, as this would infringe on consistorial power.[52]

Upon the death of Van Raalte in 1876 (who had stemmed the tide of discontent over the Masonic issue), the subsequent hard economic times for Hope College (that weakened the resolve of some as to the viability and good judgment of the RCA on the whole), and with one rabble-rousing expatriate Freemason named Edmond Ronayne (who lectured against Freemasonry in Holland in 1879), anxieties reached a fevered pitch. In 1880, a renewed overture to the General Synod from the classes of Holland and Wisconsin, joined by the classes of Grand River and Illinois and the Particular Synod of Chicago, was met with a tactical response that "no communicant member, and no minister of the Reformed Church in America ought to unite with or to remain in any society or institution, whether secret or open, whose principles and practices are anti-Christian, or contrary to the faith and practice of the Church to which he belongs."[53]

The resultant losses of RCA members and churches to the CRC in the years immediately following the 1880 General Synod response were staggering. In 1882 eight congregations left the RCA over Freemasonry. Between 1880 and 1882, the Classis of Holland alone lost 400 families, including a majority of its flagship congregation at Pillar Church.[54]

States, Masonic membership was not necessarily in contradiction with religious beliefs. In fact, as it was widely known that George Washington was a Mason (along with other founding fathers), it was considered patriotic to join a lodge. For many, especially in the East, church membership and Masonic membership was seen as the harmonious rendering of oneself to God and country.

[51] The True Reformed Protestant Dutch Church in Hackensack had done the same in 1831.
[52] *MGS* 1870, 96–97.
[53] Bruggink and Baker, *By Grace Alone* 141.
[54] For a discussion of the impact of Freemasonry on the membership and clergy of Pillar

Residual Losses are the CRC's Gains

By 1900, the CRC had swollen to 144 congregations. Expectantly, they had been joined by the remnants of the Hackensack secession in 1890. But new immigrants to the Midwest were also more inclined to join the CRC than the overtly Americanized RCA. The theological indoctrination of their native secessionist church, the Christelijke Gereformeerde Kerk, had predisposed them to the orthodoxy of the CRC. Furthermore, upon the merger of the Gereformeerde Kerk with "the highly sophisticated and powerful theological structure" of Abraham Kuyper's (1837-1920) Doleantie (sorrowing secession) in 1892, the church became endowed with a profoundly literate and education-minded constituency.[55] According to Arie Brouwer, "The immigrants who valued theological orthodoxy above all else or who regarded themselves as radical separatists affiliated with the CRC. Those who placed a premium on piety were sometimes attracted to the RCA, which had assimilated more of the hymns, literature, and beliefs of American fundamentalism."[56]

Yet she on earth hath union with God, the Three-In-One,
And mystic sweet communion with those whose rest is won;
O happy ones and holy, Lord, give us grace that we,
Like them, the meek and lowly, on high may dwell with thee.

Guidance from Our Statements of Unity

The Belgic Confession

Our four confessions—the Canons of Dort, the Belgic Confession, the Heidelberg Catechism, and the Belhar Confession—each came about after a costly struggle for religious freedom.[57] Also known as our standards of unity, the documents say as much about what we embrace as what we exclude, and from them we can glean crucial guidance in

---

Church, see Elton J. Bruins, *The Americanization of a Congregation*, The Historical Series of the Reformed Church in America 26, 2nd ed. (Grand Rapids, MI: Eerdmans, 1996), 29-35.

[55] Bruggink and Baker, *By Grace Alone* 142. For a definitive biography, see James D. Bratt and Mark A. Noll, *Abraham Kuyper: Modern Calvinist, Christian Democrat* (Grand Rapids, MI: Eerdmans, 2013).

[56] Brouwer, *Reformed Church Roots*, 127.

[57] See *Our Faith: Ecumenical Creeds, Reformed Confessions, and Other Resources* (Grand Rapids, Michigan, Faith Alive Christian Resources, 2013). See also *Liturgy and Confessions* (New York: Reformed Church Press, 1992). The Canons of Dort will not be discussed in this paper as that document does not make a statement of unity.

maintaining unity while addressing our differences today. Such was the case when Guido de Bres (1522-1567) penned the 37 articles of the Belgic Confession amidst Phillip II's (1527-1598) pogrom against the fledgling church. By the 1570s the Belgic Confession had become the cornerstone of the Reformed Church in the Netherlands. "Article 27: The Holy Catholic Church" makes this eloquent statement of unity:

> We believe and confess one single catholic or universal church—a holy congregation and gathering of true Christian believers, awaiting their entire salvation in Jesus Christ being washed by his blood, and sanctified and sealed by the Holy Spirit. This church has existed from the beginning of the world and will last until the end, as appears from the fact that Christ is eternal King who cannot be without subjects. And this holy church is preserved by God against the rage of the whole world, even though for a time it may appear very small in the eyes of men—as though it were snuffed out.
>
> For example, during the very dangerous time of Ahab the Lord preserved for himself seven thousand men who did not bend their knees to Baal [1 Kings 19:18].
>
> And so this holy church is not confined, bound, or limited to a certain place or certain persons. But it is spread and dispersed throughout the entire world, though still joined and united in heart and will, in one and the same Spirit, by the power of faith.[58]

The Heidelberg Catechism

The 129 questions of the Heidelberg Catechism were the handiwork of Zacharias Ursinus (1534–1583) and Caspar Olevianus (1536-1587) when called upon by Frederick III (1515-1576), Elector Palatine of the Rhine, to settle a schism between Lutherans and Calvinists in his region. The catechism is truly remarkable for its thorough treatment of the tenets of Calvinism (that range from the foundations of faith in Jesus Christ to the meaning of the sacraments) and for its pastoral tone. The so called "short catechism," most often in print today, is divided into three main sections: "Man's Misery," "Man's Deliverance," and "Man's Gratitude." In the "Man's Deliverance" section are two questions and answers that are particularly relevant to issues of unity:[59]

---

[58] *Liturgy and Confessions*, 29.
[59] Heidelberg Catechism, Reformed Church in America, www.rca.org/resources/heidelbergcatechism.

Q54: What do you believe concerning the "holy catholic church"?

A: I believe that the Son of God through his Spirit and Word, out of the entire human race, from the beginning of the world to its end, gathers, protects, and preserves for himself a community chosen for eternal life and united in true faith. And of this community I am and always will be a living member.

Q55: What do you understand by "the communion of saints"?

A: First, that believers one and all, as members of this community, share in Christ and in all his treasures and gifts. Second, that each member should consider it his duty to use his gifts readily and cheerfully for the service and enrichment of the other members.

The Belhar Confession

The Belhar Confession was adopted as the fourth standard of unity (or confession) by the RCA in 2010 after three years of provisional use. Originally written in Afrikaans in 1982, the confession is a Reformed statement of faith and, at its inception, a protest against a segregated society that was levied through the church. When the apartheid ended in 1994 and the Uniting Reformed Church in Southern Africa (URCSA) was formed, the unity that the confession professed as "both a gift and an obligation for the church" took on a much greater meaning than desegregation. The unity now has become a clarion call to justice for any person or group that has been wronged or ignored. Thus, God is the God of all people: rich, poor, underprivileged, or suffering in any way. Social segregation for any reason is sinful as it is the church's obligation to care for all of God's people.

> We believe that God has entrusted the church with the message of reconciliation in and through Jesus Christ, that the church is called to be the salt of the earth and the light of the world, that the church is called blessed because it is a peacemaker, and that the church is witness both by word and by deed to the new heaven and the new earth in which righteousness dwells (2 Corinthians 5:17-21; Matthew 5:13-16; Matthew 5:9; 2 Peter 3:13; Revelation 21-22).

A Final Word

Whatever our differences may be, we are called upon to make peace and live in unity by our God, who has guaranteed us salvation through the sacrifice of Jesus Christ. God alone holds the power of judgment. We keep in tension our unique aspect of being both Reformed and ecumenical. While it is sometimes a source of derision, it is more often something to be celebrated. If the above is but a history of the "growing pains" alluded to at the onset of this paper, then we shall get through the next debate as well, whatever it may be about. As Reformed people we are transformed through the loving grace of God, and are called as a transforming agent in God's name.

CHAPTER 12

Ministerial Supply, 1900–2010: A Historical Perspective[1]

Introduction

Several church leaders have called attention to an apparent shortage of ministers of Word and sacrament in the Reformed Church in America (RCA). In his general secretary's report to the 2001 General Synod, Wes Granberg-Michaelson stated that there is a shortage of ministers of Word and sacrament in the RCA. After supporting his claim with several statistics, he declared:

> Friends, those numbers don't add up. The Reformed Church in America faces an urgent challenge of calling forth pastors and leaders who can guide our congregations into future mission.[2]

The concern about an adequate supply of ministers is not new in the history of the Reformed Church in America. Ministerial supply was one of the concerns facing the denomination at the beginning of

---

[1] *Minutes of General Synod* (hereafter *MGS*) 2017 (New York: Reformed Church Press, 2017), 286-96.
[2] *MGS* 2001, 44.

the twentieth century. In 1900, the RCA's Board of Education reported 90 candidates under its care in colleges and seminaries preparing themselves for the office of minister of Word and sacrament. One year later, the number of candidates had decreased by 19, leading the Committee on Education, Academies, and Colleges to present the following resolution to the General Synod of 1901:

> That in view of the decrease in the number of students preparing for the ministry under the care of the Board, that we urge our Pastors and Churchs [sic] to press the claims of the Master for laborers in his harvest; while at the same time we heartily endorse the suggestion of the Board that there shall be a thorough preparation for the work, and no short cut into the ministry.[3]

The concern was justified. The downward trend continued until 1906 when the number of candidates stood at just 56.

By 1907, however, the prospects were improving. The number of candidates continued growing until they had reached the 1900 level of 90. The following year, even that level was surpassed. This shift from ministerial shortage to ministerial surplus is a cycle that was repeated four times in the first half of the 20th century.

History can be a tool for understanding. What understanding does the history of ministerial supply in the first half of the 20th century offer the 21st-century church?

A "Serious Condition": 1901–1906

In its annual report to the 1902 General Synod, the Board of Education observed that the number of candidates under its care in colleges and seminaries was the lowest since 1886. The number of pre-seminary candidates in colleges—28—was called "alarmingly small." The report also noted that the number of ministers serving the church for the past four years had decreased by 56 due to death. The situation was not unique to the RCA but was similar in other denominations across North America.[4]

The state of ministerial supply was called a "serious condition" by the Committee on Education, Academies, and Colleges in its report to the General Synod of 1903. The committee noted that "the number of

---

[3] *MGS* 1901, 1067.
[4] The Seventieth Annual Report of the Board of Education, RCA (1902), 3.

those enlisted for work in the Kingdom of God is far too small."[5] The situation was seen by the committee as "an index to the spiritual life of the Church" and its primary cause was to be found in "a prevailing worldly and materialistic spirit, which acts as a dry-rot in the life of the Church."[6] Accordingly, the committee urged pastors and consistories to "use prayerful effort in the direction of placing before the minds of promising and consecrated young men in their congregations, the claims of the Christian ministry."[7]

Increasing Ministerial Supply: 1907–1912

Evidently pastors and consistories took the 1903 resolution to heart, for by 1907, the tone of the board reports was changing. In its 1907 report, the Board of Education pointed out that the 21 new students that came under the care of the board was the largest for any one year in the board's history.[8] In 1910, the board was able to report that the number of candidates preparing for ministry under its care between 1905 and 1910 had increased by 50 percent.[9]

The 1910 report of the Board of Education, though generally positive in nature, did find some information disturbing: nine of the RCA classes east of Detroit (about a third of the classes in the three eastern synods) did not have any candidates in the RCA's two seminaries nor any college students under the care of the board.[10] In 1911, the Board of Education reported the largest number of candidates preparing for the ministry (90) under its care since 1900.[11]

A New Challenge: 1913–1921

After an increase in the number of candidates preparing for ministry under the care of the Board of Education from 1907 until 1912, the number again started to decline in 1913. By 1918, there were 63 candidates for the ministry under the care of the board in colleges and seminaries (plus five students preparing for service as medical

---

[5] MGS 1903, 350.
[6] MGS 1903, 350-51.
[7] MGS 1903, 351.
[8] The Seventy-Fifth Annual Report of the Board of Education of the Reformed Church in America (1907), 2.
[9] The Seventy-Eighth Annual Report of the Board of Education of the Reformed Church in America (1910), 3.
[10] Board of Education Report (1910), 3.
[11] The Seventy-Ninth Annual Report of the Board of Education of the Reformed Church in America (1911), 2.

missionaries). The impact of WWI was beginning to be reflected in the figures, as 19 candidates under the care of the board were on war leave.[12]

The report of the board for 1919 offered this summary for the decade:

> A glance at the situation for the past decade shows that during this period 211 students for the ministry were received under the care of the Board of Education. As this Board enrolls an average of 80 per cent. [sic] of the graduates of our seminaries, the number of students for the ministry of our Reformed Church, preparing in our own institutions during the past ten years, may be put at about 260, an average of 26 a year. But not all who begin to study for the ministry reach the goal. The number of students taken from the roll of the Board during the years 1909-18 was 47, or 22 per cent. [sic] of the total received. This would reduce the average number of students actually entering the ministry to about 21 a year. As the deaths of 170 of our Reformed Church ministers have been reported for the past decade, while our seminaries have recorded 173 graduates, it is clear that the growth of this part of the organism since the opening of the century has been hardly perceptible.[13]

The RCA's "Five Year Progress Campaign" had the doubling of church membership as its first goal, which, if met, meant that the church's leadership needs would also have to double. The reasoning behind this assumption failed, however, to take into account that small membership churches—more typical of many RCA congregations—would not necessarily need additional ordained pastors to care for twice the number of members. Nonetheless, the board report noted that:

> The actual need of Reformed Church ministers and other Christian leaders, in the next five years, in view of the attempted doubling of the membership, of the present meager supply, and of the call of our Board of Foreign Missions for at least 12 new missionaries for each of the next five years would point to 50 recruits a year for the ministry or 250 for the five-year period.[14]

---

[12] The Eighty-Sixth Annual Report of the Board of Education of the Reformed Church in America (1918), 2.
[13] The Eighty-Seventh Annual Report of the Board of Education of the Reformed Church in America, 1919, 5.
[14] Board of Education Report, 1919, 5.

The Fifth Annual Report of the Progress Campaign Committee in 1923 showed an increase in communicant membership from 134,039 in 1918 to 143,475 in 1923, a gain of 9,436 (about seven percent).[15]

In order to meet the projected leadership needs for the five-year period of the campaign, the board calculated that each existing RCA congregation would have to recruit at least one candidate for the ministry.[16] The number of candidates preparing for the ministry under the care of the Board of Education increased from 68 in 1918 to 92 in 1923, an increase of 35 percent.[17]

The vacancy rate in churches in 1920 was reported at 20 to 25 percent.[18] By 1921, there was growing concern about a shortage of ministerial candidates in the RCA. The Board of Education's report to the 1921 General Synod observed that the ranks of ministry were "sadly depleted" and called the scarcity of candidates for ministry "appalling."[19]

From Shortage to Surplus, Again: 1926–1935

By the middle of the decade, it was reported that the student body at New Brunswick Theological Seminary had "increased quite materially" and that members of the senior class had all found placements. Nonetheless, it was asserted that two or three times their number could have been placed.[20] One year later, there was a growing sense that the RCA had an adequate supply of ministerial candidates. In some areas, there were reports of anxiety about the possibility that the ministry had become "overcrowded."[21]

Ten years after a shortage of ministerial candidates had been reported, one finds in the Board of Education report that "There is a pronounced unemployment problem in the ministry."[22] A rise in seminary enrollment over that ten-year period was noted as a possible

---

[15] *MGS* 1923, 209.
[16] Board of Education Report, 1919, 5–6.
[17] *MGS* 1923, 209.
[18] The One Hundredth Annual Report of the Board of Education of the Reformed Church in America (1931), 11.
[19] The Eighty-Ninth Annual Report of the Board of Education of the Reformed Church in America (1921), 11.
[20] The Ninety-Fifth Annual Report of the Board of Education of the Reformed Church in America (1926), 5.
[21] The Ninety-Sixth Annual Report of the Board of Education of the Reformed Church in America (1927), 6–7.
[22] Board of Education Report (1931), 11.

factor in the change in the supply of ministerial candidates. The RCA was not the only denomination facing an over-supply of ministerial candidates.[23]

One reason for the change in the ministerial supply picture is the attention given to recruitment by the Board of Education. In the 1920s, the annual report of the Board of Education began to reflect an emphasis on recruiting candidates for the ministry. Starting with the annual report for 1924, a special section of the report was entitled "Recruitment" or "Recruiting for the Ministry." This heading appeared in Board of Education reports until 1927 and then disappeared until 1931.

In 1920, the first "Life Work Conference" was held in New Brunswick. The two-day conference was attended by almost 100 people, including Rutgers College students and high school students. The conference was organized by the Society of Inquiry, a student association at New Brunswick Theological Seminary.[24] In March of 1922, a second Life Work Conference, attended by 121 participants, was held at New Brunswick Theological Seminary. Of the registered participants, 63 came from outside of New Brunswick, and 32 from Rutgers College and Preparatory School for Men.[25] Life Work Conferences were also held in 1924 and 1926 (plans for a conference to be held at Hope College in 1927 were abandoned).

In 1922, the General Synod also gave its approval for making the first Sunday in May "Vocation Sunday." Various resources were prepared for use by pastors in preaching and other activities. "Ministerial Vignettes" were published in publications such as the *Christian Intelligencer* and *De Hope*.

Given the increase in the number of ministerial candidates over the decade, by 1929 "recruitment" had been replaced by "The Bureau of Pastoral Exchange and Supply" as a heading in the Board of Education's annual report.

If the 1920s were marked by a preoccupation with the recruitment of ministerial candidates, the early 1930s were marked by a shift in focus from quantity to quality. In their report to the 1932 General Synod, the Board of Education noted that:

---

[23] The One Hundred and First Annual Report of the Board of Education of the Reformed Church in America (1932), 6.

[24] The Eighty-Eighth Annual Report of the Board of Education of the Reformed Church in America (1920), 7.

[25] The Ninetieth Annual Report of the Board of Education of the Reformed Church in America (1922), 5.

> The churches are well manned with ministers. Many congregations which, ten years ago, found it impossible to secure ministers now have settled pastors. In many a classis it is not possible to find a vacant congregation capable of calling a pastor, even with the aid of the Board of Domestic Missions—if indeed that Board had even the necessarily modest amount to appropriate. We are in that condition which may be observed from a study of the statistics to which we come around, on the average, about three times in a century. From the point of view of the numbers, we have an over-supply of ministers. Practically every denomination faces the same situation. There are more ministers today than there are churches.[26]

The report also suggested that there be no "short cuts" to the office of minister of Word and sacrament.[27]

The Board of Education report for 1933 devoted significant attention to the issue of "ministerial opportunity." The report presented two graphs—one tracing the number of students under the care of the board and another (a "Chart of Ministerial Opportunity") tracing the vacancy rate in congregations between 1833 and 1933 (see Appendix A and Appendix B). The report offered several observations based on the data in these charts: 1) when the vacancy rate in congregations is 10 percent or less, opportunities for pastors seeking a change or seminary graduates seeking a placement are "increasingly difficult," 2) when the vacancy rate in congregations is 15 to 20 percent, there is greater "ministerial opportunity," 3) that for about 70 of the years between 1833 and 1933, the vacancy rate in RCA congregations was between 15 and 20 percent, 4) when the vacancy rate in churches dropped below 15 percent, it was usually for short periods of time, 5) the 1933 vacancy rate of eight percent was the lowest for a whole century, 6) from 1833 to 1933, there was a gradual but steady downward trend in "ministerial opportunity," 7) the vacancy rate would increase again shortly, 8) the decline in the percentage of vacant churches between 1893 and 1898 coincided with a large enrollment in the seminaries, with the number of graduates offsetting the number of deaths of ministers, 9) a similar decline in the number of vacancies in churches between 1920 and 1932 corresponded with an increase in seminary enrollment, and 10) an increase in the supply of ministers tended to coincide with periods of

---

[26] Board of Education Report (1932), 5–6.
[27] Board of Education Report (1932); 7.

national and global economic depression.[28]

The "pronounced unemployment problem" reported in 1931 continued well into the decade. In 1934, the Board of Education reported that the seminaries were experiencing difficulty in placing graduates.

> Twenty-six men are graduating from the two institutions. Our churches are so well supplied with ministers that there are few places for the seminary graduates. Many suggestions have been made as to ways in which these young men may be used. The situation, however, is unchanged at the time of writing this Report, hence we are still at the suggestion stage.[29]

Toward the end of the 1930s, the Board of Education reported that the number of college students under its care who were preparing for the ministry was again decreasing. The board's report for 1938 stated:

> Attention was called in the report of this Board last year to the fact that the number of students in preparation for the ministry in colleges was decreasing and the suggestion was made that the claims of the ministry should be pressed again, particular attention being given to making the appeal to specially promising young men in our churches. The demands upon the ministry today are tremendous and only the best equipped survive the strain.[30]

The very next year, however, one reads about "the rising tide of ministerial candidates." The Board of Education's report for 1939 observed again the connection between the economy and the available supply of ministers:

> It will be noted that periods of economic depression are accompanied by a larger number of candidates for the ministry while periods of prosperity always bring with them a diminution in this supply. The present continued depression is running true

---

[28] The One Hundred and Second Annual Report of the Board of Education of the Reformed Church in America (1933), 7–8.

[29] The One Hundred and Third Annual Report of the Board of Education of the Reformed Church in America (1934), 4.

[30] The One Hundredth and Seventh Annual Report of the Board of Education of the Reformed Church in America (1938), 8.

to form in this respect at least.[31]

Asking ministers to retire who had reached the age of 70 was one suggestion for addressing the problem of ministerial oversupply.[32]

The Impact of War: 1941–1948

War, like economics, also impacted the RCA's ministerial supply in the first half of the 20th century. During the First World War, the number of candidates preparing for the ministry under the care of the Board of Education dropped from 89 in 1917 (the year in which the United States entered WWI) to 68 in 1918 and 1919. The total war program of the 1940s had an even greater impact—the number of candidates preparing for the ministry in 1944 had dropped to 49 from 93 in 1940 (a 47.3 percent decrease compared to the 23.6 percent decrease from 1917 to 1918). With alarm, the board report for 1944 noted, "The number of students in colleges preparing for the ministry under the care of this Board is at the lowest point in 60 years!"[33]

Several options for responding to the ministerial supply crisis were noted in the 1944 report. They included relaxing requirements of candidates preparing for the ministry, asking churches with multiple staff members to release assistant pastors for calls to vacant churches, and pressing gifted elders and deacons into service. The report asks,

> Is it not feasible, however, for the purpose of furnishing leadership for our churches, to revive the time-honored custom in the Reformed Church of calling upon gifted elders and deacons to assume some of these necessary duties of the pastor, such as conducting church services "for the duration"?[34]

By 1946, the number of students under the care of the Board of Education had dropped to 25. The report noted:

> It will however be seen that the need for the discovery of leadership candidates for the church is one of serious concern. The Board of Foreign Missions alone needs some sixty candidates for the mission fields in the next several years. And although returning

---

[31] The One Hundred and Eighth Annual Report of the Board of Education of the Reformed Church in America (1939), 20.
[32] Board of Education Report (1939) 20.
[33] Annual Report of the Board of Education, RCA (1944), 4.
[34] Board of Education, Report (1944) 4.

chaplains have serviced to staff a large number of our many pastorless [sic] churches, and others will, still there is great need for highly qualified ministerial candidates.[35]

The report emphasized the need for "highly qualified" candidates: "We need young men and women today for the ministry and mission field who are intellectually competent, mentally alert, who possess cultural awareness and curiosity, and who, although still young, exhibit a strong professional responsibility in the direction of their proposed services."[36] It was not enough for a candidate to be simply devout. The report for 1947 expressed optimism with regard to the prospects for meeting the leadership needs of the church, noting that 177 young men and women had expressed interest in ministry or other forms of full-time Christian service.[37]

The Board of Education had begun the 20th century with an enrollment of 90 candidates under its care. In 1950, the Board of Education was once more able to report 90 candidates under its care in colleges and seminaries preparing for the office of minister of Word and sacrament. The cycles had come full circle.

The 1950 General Synod Report on the State of Religion offered a century-long perspective on churches and ministers (See Table 1 below).

Table 1[38]

	1850	1900	1925	1950	Gain
Churches	292	643	730	763	161%
Ministers	293	715	809	884	201%

A Time of Growth and Increase in Ministerial Supply: 1950–1990

In his report to the 1969 General Synod, the president of General Synod noted concerns about the future of the ministry in the Reformed Church.[39] In response, the General Synod decided "to continue in greater depth its study of the whole problem of recruitment for and retention in the parish ministry."[40] In 1973, a report was presented to General Synod as a joint project of the coordinator of human resources (Office of Human Resources) and the director of professional development

---

[35] Annual Report of the Board of Education, RCA (1946), 12–13.
[36] Board of Education, Report (1946), 13.
[37] Annual Report of the Board of Education, RCA (1947), 5.
[38] Report on the State of Religion (1950), 239.
[39] *MGS* 1969, 319.
[40] *MGS* 1969, R-1, 330.

(Board of Theological Education). Among other things, this report examined probable retirement of ministers in the following decade, a view of the decade prior of numbers of churches and ministers, and the number of new ministers needed to maintain supply.

It was determined that in order to maintain the supply of ministers, figuring in projected retirements over the next ten years, there would need to be 28 to 35 new ministers entering the pastorate for the next ten years.[41] This report also gave a series of charts, one of which was a comparison of churches and ministers from 1962–1971, which is very illustrative for our purposes (see Table 2).

Table 2[42]

Year	Churches	Ministers
1962	907	1,152
1963	913	1,171
1964	921	1,175
1965	922	1,201
1966	927	1,203
1967	934	1,234
1968	939	1,276
1969	939	1,271
1970	935	1,291
1971	939	1,298

While there may be some variance in methodologies between the previous two tables, one thing is clear: there was a significant increase in ministers between 1950 and 1962, from 884 in 1950 to 1,152 in 1962, an increase of more than 30 percent, while the number of churches in that 12-year period increased by just under 19 percent. Simply by looking at these raw numbers (even allowing for some variance in statistical methodologies), it is clear that the decade of the 1950s was a period of significant growth in both churches and ministers, with growth in ministers outpacing that of churches.

Additionally, from this it is clear that for the period of 1962–1971, the trend in both churches and ministers is upward. Indeed, the report noted that the number of churches increased 3.5 percent while the number of ministers increased 12.7 percent for the same period. And further, in order to facilitate the movement of ministers, it was

---

[41] *MGS* 1973, 141.
[42] *MGS* 1973, 141.

determined that it is ideal for there to be a ten percent vacancy rate among churches.[43]

The question of ministerial supply appears relatively quiet in the synodical record for the next decade, returning again in 1983 when the Advisory Committee on Church Vocations recommended that the Office of Human Resources, among other things, "assess the potential opportunity for professional ministry likely to become available in the RCA between 1985 and 1990."[44]

In its report to the 1984 General Synod, the Office of Human Resources noted, "Initially, this study only underlines what we have known for years; namely, that we produce more clergy than we can possibly assimilate in the parish."[45] Rather than a shortage, the problem was having an abundance of ministers to support adequate employment and movement of ministers.

> To what and for what are we recruiting? A theological education does not guarantee life-time employment. It is important to be honest with the person who professes interest in ministry; and while we do not wish to impede the moving of the Holy Spirit in a person's life, we should also indicate that prospects for employment in a church are not without limits.[46]

It was also noted that the number of churches who cannot afford a full-time minister was increasing and there must be an openness to recognizing ministry beyond full-time parish ministry as this will not be a reality for many ministers or people entering the ministry.[47] Furthermore, the General Synod of 1984 considered a proposal that was, in essence, the commissioned pastor but with a different name. This was rejected, among other reasons, because it "would make the present over-supply of ministers even worse."[48]

Indeed, in 1980, there were 930 churches and 1,240 non-retired active ministers.[49] This surplus of ministers did not decrease in the following decade, but in fact increased, as there were 960 churches

---

[43] *MGS* 1973, 140.
[44] *MGS* 1983, 237.
[45] *MGS* 1984, 203.
[46] *MGS* 1984, 204–05.
[47] *MGS* 1984, 205.
[48] *MGS* 1984, 182.
[49] The term "non-retired active ministers" includes RCA ministers of all designations except retired or inactive ministers.

in 1990 and 1,438 non-retired active ministers in the same year. The number of churches increased approximately 3.23 percent during the decade from 1980 to 1990, while the number of ministers increased approximately 16 percent during the same period.

Small Decrease: 1990–2000

The decade following 1990 saw small decreases in both the number of churches and ministers, though nothing that could remotely be considered a shortage of ministers. The number of non-retired active ministers decreased by about 3.13 percent (from approximately 1,438 ministers in 1990 to approximately 1,393 ministers in 2000); however, it must be remembered that the number of churches also decreased by approximately 2.19 percent during the same period (from 960 to 939). Despite these decreases, however, the numbers show that there were still enough ministers in the Reformed Church in America to adequately supply the churches.

Ministerial Surplus and Perceived Shortage: 2000–2010

In 2000, the General Synod's Advisory Committee on Church Vocations brought a new recommendation to the floor, which was subsequently approved by the General Synod.

> To instruct the General Synod Council to do an impact study regarding the potential lack of ministry leadership in the Reformed Church in America in the next five years and determine possible courses of action to provide qualified leadership for all areas of ministry in the Reformed Church in America.[50]

The committee's reasoning was that "Current statistics indicate that all areas of RCA ministry will be facing an urgent need to find qualified leaders in the next five years."[51] At the time, however, no further data was presented to support such a claim.

In 2001, both the president of General Synod and the general secretary made reference to a survey that came out of this study which showed that 182 congregations, "almost 20 percent," were without a full-time minister, and that for more than one-third of those churches, resource limitations provided little prospect of being able to call a full-time minister in the foreseeable future.[52] Furthermore, the report

---

[50] *MGS* 2000, 350.
[51] *MGS* 2000, 350.
[52] *MGS* 2001, 35.

continued to project retirements and new minister projections, and estimated that there could be upward of "29 percent of our churches without full-time ordained pastors. It is not an exaggeration to say that we are teetering on the edge of a full-blown crisis."[53] In the interpretation of the data, the term "clergy shortage" was used as a basis for arguing that the preaching elder designation, already in existence, was insufficient and a new designation was needed.[54] The general secretary, in his report to the General Synod, used the same data to argue that there was an insufficient number of ministers to fulfill the need, and with the "plans to start 182 new churches over the next ten years" more ministers would be needed in order to fulfill the need that was to come.[55]

The next year, the president of General Synod 2002 made the same claim of a shortage of ministers, citing the same number of "[a]lmost 20 percent of our churches are experiencing difficulty finding ordained ministers of Word and sacrament to serve as their pastors."[56] While there was a problem to be addressed, a shortage of ministers was not it. Indeed, from the data presented, the conclusion of a minister shortage seems to have been a gross misrepresentation that served to bolster support for the establishment of the previously rejected designation, which would become known in 2002 as the commissioned pastor.

While there may have been a season of slightly higher rates of vacancy, the numbers in no way support any hint of a shortage of ministers. Indeed, there were reports of ministers and candidates for ministry without calls.[57] While the concept of a minister shortage appears for several years in the synodical record as a fact, the raw numbers show something very different.

Furthermore, the projected shortage not only never materialized, it could be argued that the surplus increased. The projected shortage was dependent, primarily, upon three factors: increasing retirements, decreasing numbers of seminary graduates, and an increase in the number of churches. The numbers, however, do not support this hypothesis. To be sure, the economic downturn in this decade likely pushed some ministers, who may have otherwise retired, to remain in active service. However, this cannot completely explain the difference. In the decade from 2000 to 2010, the number of churches decreased by

[53] *MGS* 2001, 35.
[54] *MGS* 2001, 36.
[55] *MGS* 2001, 44.
[56] *MGS* 2002, 35.
[57] Eric Titus, "'No' to Commissioned Pastors," *The Church Herald*, February 2004, 6; Corstian DeVos, "Flak and Flattery," *The Church Herald*, April 2004, 4–5.

about 1.6 percent (from 939 to 924), while the number of non-retired active ministers increased by about 8.9 percent (from approximately 1,393 to approximately 1,517). To put this in another perspective, in 1980, when the concern was the surplus of ministers, there were approximately 1.33 non-retired active ministers per church. In 2010, there were approximately 1.64 non-retired active ministers per church, which is an even greater surplus, not a shortage. Indeed, the 30-year trend for numbers of churches is stable, while the trend for ministerial supply is upward (see Table 3).

Table 3

	1980	1990	2000	2010	Percent increase/ (decrease)
Ministers	1,240	1,438	1,393	1,517	22.34%
Churches	930	960	939	924	(0.65%)

Conclusion

This brief study of ministerial supply in the 20th century yields several observations:

- There are cycles of shortage and surplus in the supply of ministerial candidates.
- These cycles are affected by economic conditions (shortage in good economic times and surplus in poor economic times) and by war.
- High standards for ministerial candidates were maintained throughout the 20th century despite the shortages in ministerial supply.
- Recruitment efforts were effective.
- Shortages can be perceived as real even when they are not.

What lessons may be taken from this survey of ministerial supply in the RCA? One lesson is that there are cycles of shortage and surplus. The current "crisis," whether real or perceived, is not the whole picture. The cyclical nature of ministerial supply needs to be recognized in conversations about any ministerial shortage. Strategic thought needs to be given to the "surplus" side of the cycle and its implications for theological education, the placement of graduates, and the movement of ministers.

This cyclical pattern appears to be influenced by economic conditions and by war. This points to a second lesson: the forces affecting ministerial shortage and surplus are complex, and conversations about the current ministerial shortage need to be more nuanced. Vacancies alone cannot be used to defend claims of ministerial shortage; economic conditions within the churches must also be taken into consideration. Single-factor explanations and simple solutions will not produce effective or lasting strategies.

An emphasis on recruitment and on high standards are recurring themes throughout the first decades of the 20th century as the denomination experienced repeated cycles of an under- and over-supply of ministerial candidates. This emphasis on the quality of candidates for the office of minister of Word and sacrament is another lesson this survey offers. Ministers who are thought to have lower abilities than others (which is often an extremely subjective idea) tend to find ministry placements during periods of true shortage, but often find themselves without a charge in times of surplus.

A fourth lesson involves the kinds of strategies the church employed when faced with a shortage of ministerial candidates. In addition to approving resolutions urging parents, pastors, and congregations to recruit candidates for ministry, concrete actions were taken, such as the Life Work Conference and Vocation Sunday. The Wolfert Conferences of the 1960s are one example of how an earlier strategy was adopted for a new era of recruitment.

A fifth lesson speaks to the strength of perceptions even when they contradict reality. Since 1950, there has not been a true shortage of ministers. There may have been seasons when there were more vacant churches than average or when there were churches that could not afford a full-time minister, but this does not mean that there existed a shortage of ministers. Indeed, more often than not, there was an abundance of ministers to support the churches. Simply because it is assumed to be real does not make it real.

This survey of one period in the history of the RCA suggests that the narrative about ministerial shortages needs to be challenged and the perspective needs to be broadened. The Reformed Church in America is excellent at keeping records, statistics, and data. We need to be sure that our conclusions are based on good data and information rather than simply adopting the narratives and enthusiasms of the moment, and that we do not make significant and lasting (and, in particular, constitutional) changes based upon these momentary enthusiasms.

Future Work

This is but a brief snapshot of a much larger picture. A more comprehensive study on ministerial supply, retirement, ministers dismissed and received, and new candidates entering ministry is certainly warranted and would be exceedingly valuable.

Appendix A[58]

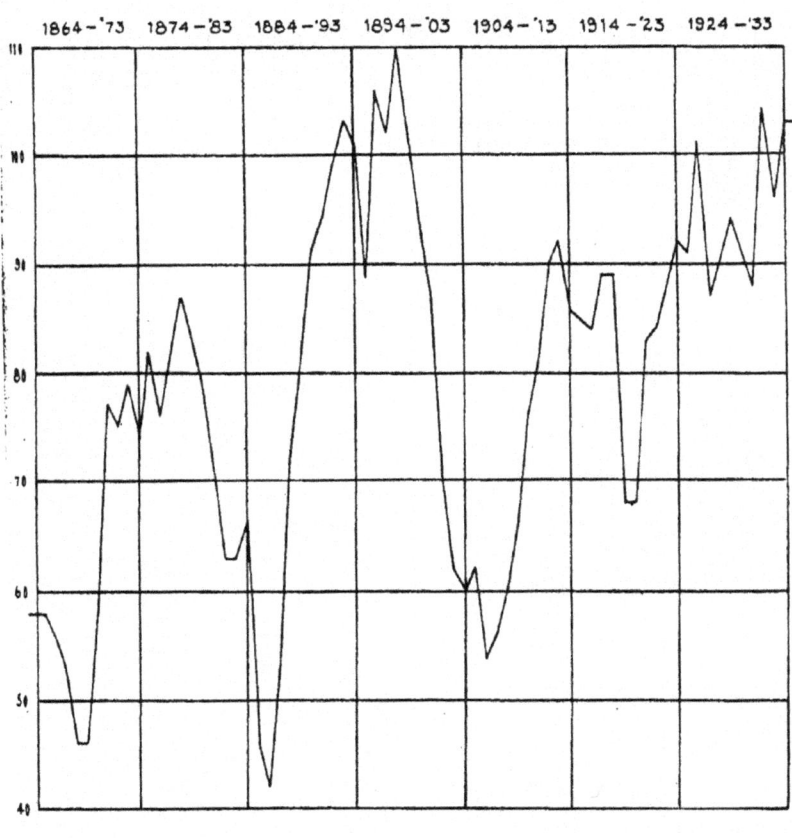

GRAPH NO. 1

---

[58] Board of Education Report (1933), 3.

Appendix B[59]

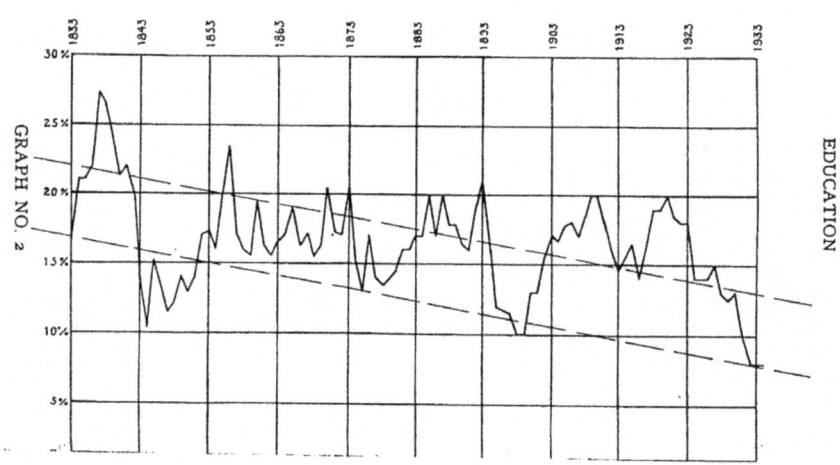

[59] Board of Education Report (1933), 6.

CHAPTER 13

"Historic and Faithful Witnesses": Reflecting on the Standards and How They Have Been Used in the Forms of Declaration and the Church[1]

Since the 2017 General Synod passed R 17-29—"To affirm that the Heidelberg Catechism Q&A 108 and 109 categorically states [sic] that God condemns 'all unchastity,' which includes same-sex sexual activity, and that faithful adherence to the RCA's Standards, therefore, entails the affirmation that marriage is between one man and one woman"[2] — there have been concerns expressed about what this means for ministers and General Synod professors. Bearers of these two offices, as well as licensed candidates for ministry under care of classes, are unique in the RCA for being required to subscribe to a Form of Declaration that states: "I accept the Standards as historic and faithful witnesses to the Word of God."[3]

The primary question seems to be whether, given this wording of the forms, the interpretation affirmed by the 2017 Synod can be used to

---

[1] *Minutes of General Synod* (hereafter *MGS*) 2018 (New York: Reformed Church Press, 2018), 281–84.
[2] *MGS* 2017, 161.
[3] Formularies 1, 3, and 7, *Book of Church Order*, 2017 ed. (New York: Reformed Church Press, 2017), 129, 130–31, 134–35.

discipline candidates, ministers, and General Synod professors. What exactly is meant by "historic and faithful" in the Forms of Declaration? A brief historic examination of this wording and its use by the Reformed Church in America seems to be in order.

The phrase "historic and faithful" has only been part of the declarations since 1972. The change came in response to overtures from the classes of Queens and Bergen, which expressed concerns over the forms and what they said about the place of sixteenth-century doctrinal statements in a late-twentieth-century context. Queens Classis stated its reasoning as follows:

> Christianity is an [sic] historical religion, rooted in the long history of God's mighty acts, culminating in His mightiest act in Christ Jesus, and we affirm with joy the part the Reformed Church has played in the long history of God's dealing with His people.
>
> However, as God's covenant people we are a pilgrim people, called as was Abram to go from our father's house to a land that God will show us, confident that when we arrive, God will be there ahead of us.
>
> This requirement that we be a pilgrim people means that we be open always to the activity of the Holy Spirit as He may require us to re-think and re-state our theological position, and we must therefore hold with honor, but hold with open minds, the theological statements which served our fathers so well 400 years ago, ready if the Spirit requires, to re-state these pronouncements. We do not reject our history but rather affirm our openness to the leading of the Holy Spirit in our own day.[4]

The Classis of Bergen took a somewhat different reasoning:

1. The Form of Declaration for Licensed Candidates, the Form of Declaration for Ministers and the Form of Declaration for Professors of Theology all contain statements which imply that the Standards of the Reformed Church in America are equated with the Word of God. Statements include "We believe the gospel of the grace of God in Christ Jesus as revealed in the Holy Scriptures of the Old and New Testaments, and as truly set forth in the Standards of the Reformed Church in America," (the Form of Declaration for Licensed Candidates and the Form of Declaration for Ministers) and "We believe

---

[4] *MGS* 1970, 82–83.

that these Standards agree with the Word of God ..." (the Form of Declaration for Professors of Theology). While some might place the Standards on the same level as the Scriptures, it is not right to force a person who believes that the Scriptures are the normative witness to the Word of God to assent to this statement.

2. What may have been a witness to the Word of God in one particular Historical setting may not be a witness to the Word of God in a new historical setting. For example: in order to combat the abuse made of the use of images in the churches, the Heidelberg Catechism poses the following question and gives the following answer: "But may not pictures be tolerated in churches as books for the laity? (question 98) Answer— No ..." Because of a particular political situation, the Belgic Confession of Faith makes the following statement in regard to church-state relations: "and their (magistrates) office is, not only to have regard unto and watch for the welfare of the civil state, but also that they protect the sacred ministry, and thus may remove and prevent all idolatry and false worship." (Article XXXVI) The entirety of the Canons of the Synod of Dort is based upon a philosophical presupposition of Determinism which led to such statements as "... Some only, are elected, while others are passed by in the eternal decree; whom God, out of his sovereign, most just, irreprehensible and unchangeable good pleasure, hath decreed to leave in the common misery into which they have willfully plunged themselves ..." (Article XV) Are such statements still a witness to the Word of God in today's life-situation?

3. While we should acknowledge that the Standards of the Reformed Church in America did speak to a certain group of people at a certain time in a particular historical setting, we do not have to hold that they speak to men today in the same way. If statements in the Declarations prove to be stumbling blocks to brethren who cannot assent to them because of conscience and the Word of God, these stumbling blocks must be removed![5]

The matter was referred to the Commission on Theology, whose report to the 1971 General Synod did a masterful job of exploring the

---

[5] *MGS* 1970, 83–85. The Bergen overture also let the synod know that these two classes had taken steps to alter or amend the forms.

historical understanding of the place of the Standards in the life of the church.⁶

> *The Purpose of Standards*: The Reformed Church is an evangelical confessional church in the historic sense. This means that we are one of those branches of Protestantism which has distinguished itself from the Roman Church (and from some other Protestant bodies) by subscribing to an evangelical statement (or statements) of faith as the basis for our unity. The intent of such standards of unity has varied greatly among the confessional churches and in our own tradition as well. Subscription to a standard may be understood as a witness of that body to its understanding of the faith without any controversial or polemical intent. In the time of the Reformation and the century following, however, such standards were nearly always intended as a means of distinguishing the body which accepted them from other Christian bodies which held other viewpoints. As such, these standards were also symbols of disunity within the Body of Christ, professing to distinguish the true church from the false church.
>
> This polemical intent inevitably led to a second purpose and use of standards: discipline. Since they were understood to embody the right doctrine (orthodoxy), they could also be used to distinguish heresy and consequently become the basis for excluding from the body those who did not conform. The history of the Reformed Churches reveals numerous such uses and some still favor such use today.
>
> The main stream of Reformed tradition, however, has not understood the standards in this way. We have not claimed an exclusive corner on the truth. We have not viewed those outside our tradition as apostate, but considered other traditions as viable expressions of the Faith and other communions as fellow members of the Body of Christ. We have tended to look upon our standards as faithful witnesses to the Word of God to which we give our hearty consent, without making them binding upon our consciences as of divine authority.
>
> *Relationship to Scripture*: The above leads naturally to a consideration of the relationship between the standards and the

---

⁶ "The Standards" here refers to the Heidelberg Catechism and its Compendium, the Belgic Confession, and the Canons of the Synod of Dort. The Belhar Confession was not added to the Standards until 2009.

Scriptures. We hardly need to remind ourselves that the battle cry of the Reformation was *sola Scriptura*! (Scripture only) In reaction to the encroachments of Roman tradition upon the Christian conscience, the reformers took their stand upon Scripture as the sole authority— the rule (measuring stick) of faith and life. We still give loud assent to this principle today as the *raison d'etre* of the churches of the Reformation. Yet in the heat of battle in the centuries following the Reformation, Protestants found themselves invoking their standards in as final a way as any Romanist and with an authority which equalled or even surpassed that of the Scriptures.

Thus we see an ambivalence in our own tradition. On the one hand, we affirm the supreme and sole authority of Scripture. On the other hand, we have at times made the standards equally binding upon the Christian conscience. This ambivalence is enshrined in the Government of the R.C.A. ... This still does not answer the basic question, however: What is the proper place of the standards in the life of the church? How do they unite us with one another and separate us from other Christians?[7]

The commission went on to argue that the extreme positions— either that the Standards were irrelevant historical curiosities or that they were the final determination of orthodoxy for all time—must be rejected and advocated for a middle way based on the following principles:

1. The Standards must always be subordinate and subservient to Scripture. "Scripture alone can be the measure of our faith and life as Christians. ... This means no statement of faith, however faithful to the Scriptures, can be placed on a par with the Word of God."
2. The Standards are historical documents. "As such, they are the products of their times and the circumstances which produced them ... we must take note that the century which produced them was different from our time in some significant ways. ... We are called upon to bear the good news in contexts that would be utterly foreign to the 17th century Christian."
3. A Standard must have usefulness in the church. "It must be an effective teaching aid within the church, and an effective

---

[7] *MGS* 1971, 212–13.

witness to the world of the meaning of the Christian faith in our day."[8]

The commission concluded—and the synod affirmed by accepting their report and the recommendation to add the "historic and faithful" clause to the Forms of Declaration— that the Standards were faithful to Scripture as witnesses to the Word of God, but that they were "three among many witnesses to the faith ... understood as defining what is the Reformed tradition and what our fathers understood to be a faithful statement ..." and that they are "limited in their applicability to our day by the difference between the historical circumstances in which they arose and those in which we live."[9]

The understanding that led to calling our Standards "historic and faithful witnesses" clearly includes the idea that we cannot expect them to comprehend or respond to modern scientific and/or sociological situations. We also cannot bind those who read and sign the forms to be binding themselves to some strict adherence to sixteenth-century— or even late twentieth-century—concepts of sociology, science, or even theology. Nor are they meant to be disciplinary tools. Ministers, professors, and candidates are promising to engage the Standards— acknowledging their limitations—as they wrestle with the Scriptures, listening for the Word of God.

---

[8] *MGS* 1971, 214.
[9] *MGS* 1971, 214–15.

SECTION 4: CHURCH AND WORLD

CHAPTER 14

A Historical Summary of the Actions of the General Synod with Regard to Homosexuality: 1974-2012[1]

The first time that the General Synod of the Reformed Church in America was asked to consider anything expressly related to homosexuality was in the report of the Commission on Christian Action (CCA) to the synod of 1974. The social environment had clearly changed. For example, in the Stonewall Uprising of June 1969 in New York City, gays rose up against police brutality and police inattention to assaults on homosexual people. This began a movement of gay persons and their allies, organizing to seek equal protection under the law.

In this changing society, the CCA raised the matter in the church through a report focused on the injustice and abandonment experienced by persons "who are rejected because of their homosexual identity."[2] The matter of justice was central in the church's conversation from the beginning.

General Synod's primary response in 1974 was to "affirm the biblical teaching against the practice of homosexuality." Asked by the

---

[1] *Minutes of General Synod* (hereafter *MGS*) 2013 (New York: Reformed Church Press, 2013), 334-40.
[2] *MGS* 1974, 222.

CCA to encourage churches to "continue the study of homosexuality as it relates to the life and work of the church" and "to provide the compassionate acceptance of such persons within the life and mission of the church," Synod deleted the request to affirm "compassionate acceptance of such persons."[3] Thus, General Synod's direction was no more than an assertion regarding the witness of Scripture. Synod took no action on pastoral care regarding homosexual individuals.

In 1976, the CCA returned to the matter of justice for homosexual persons in a four-page report that was influenced by Robert W. Wood's book *Christ and the Homosexual*.[4] The commission's report, "The Church and the Homosexual," cites the Dutch [Heidelberg] Catechism and quotes Lewis Maddocks of the United Church of Christ: "The church has failed at the most basic level in its dealing with the homosexual by failing to recognize him [sic] as a human being who is sacred in the sight of God." The report states:

> What is unnatural to me is natural to them, however it developed, and as a result, a heterosexual encounter would be as repugnant to them as a homosexual experience would be to me. The question of "accepting" the homosexual is not one of advocacy, but of coming to terms with him or her on the basis of what is claimed to be an unalterable condition. Nor is it a question of putting a stamp of approval on promiscuity, which is to be rejected in both the straight and the gay world.[5]

The 1976 CCA proposed that the RCA "go on record upholding the right of all persons, including homosexuals, to full civil rights and especially under the law; and that no person shall be discriminated against in jobs, schools, housing, or any other employment or housing opportunity because of sexual orientation." This recommendation was tabled, and the synod voted instead, upon a motion from the floor, "to instruct the Christian Action Commission to suggest guidelines on methods for the church—local and corporate—to make a responsive attack on the devastating effects of pornography on our present culture."[6]

---

[3] *MGS* 1974, 222.
[4] Robert W. Wood, *Christ and the Homosexual: Some Observations* (New York: Vantage Press, 1960).
[5] *MGS* 1976, 193–94.
[6] *MGS* 1976, 192–95.

In 1977, during the report of the CCA, a motion was made and supported "that the 1977 General Synod go on record affirming the human and civil rights of homosexuals and lesbians."[7] On this motion, the synod voted "to refer the above motion to the Theological Commission for study and recommendation to the General Synod of 1978."[8]

In 1978, the Commission on Theology submitted a careful, eleven-and-a-half-page study paper entitled "Homosexuality: A Biblical and Theological Appraisal."[9] The synod received the report and recommended that it "be made available to the churches of the Reformed Church in America for study."[10]

The 1978 Commission on Theology's report begins by stating:

> Any responsible inquiry concerning the biblical perspective on homosexuality requires careful consideration of a new, emerging theological context. Speaking from within this context are committed Christian persons...whose biblical exegesis and theological reflection leads them to the opinion that a homosexual relationship may express the divine will for human life. Heretofore, that possibility was not considered. Paul, Luther, Calvin, and, more recently, Karl Barth assumed the sinfulness of homosexuality without question. Given the issues raised in the homosexual context, this assumption must give way to a careful re-examination of the scriptural witness in this matter.[11]

The report proceeds to examine "explicit biblical references" in a scholarly evaluation. Additionally, in faithfulness to the Second Article of the Belgic Confession, the report also provides a survey of applicable data from "the human sciences," reflecting the scientific understanding of homosexuality in 1978. The report:

1. Differentiates between same-sex attraction and acts which are innate and those which are the result of choice.
2. Recognizes the unchangeable character of basic sexuality.
3. Confesses that Scripture did not and could not speak to the situation of those persons who are innately attracted to persons of the same sex.

---

[7] *MGS* 1977, 204.
[8] *MGS* 1977, 205.
[9] *MGS* 1978, 229–40.
[10] *MGS* 1978, 240.
[11] *MGS* 1978, 229.

4. Is clear that the church's pastoral care for persons who are innately homosexual must be different from its pastoral care for heterosexual persons who freely choose same sex relationships.
5. Leaves the definition of that pastoral care of those who are "innately" homosexual for a report to be presented to the synod of 1979.

In 1979, the commission submitted an eight-page report proposing, as promised in their 1978 report, a program of "Christian Pastoral Care for the Homosexual."[12] The commission's summary of past approaches in many churches is this:

> The story of the church's dealings with the homosexual is mostly a story of ignorance, ineptitude, and ill will. For centuries, both the church and society have used legal punishment and severe moral censure [in an attempt] to control or eradicate homosexuality. The approach proved worse than useless, and in employing it the church denied its essential nature and failed the homosexual.[13]

After asserting a difference between persons for whom same-sex love is innate to their being and persons who are essentially heterosexual but choose homosexuality, the commission then went on to write its program for pastoral care as if no such distinction exists. As with the 1978 report, the 1979 report was made available to congregations for study.[14] No other official status was given to the report.

Even though the 1978 and 1979 reports of the Commission on Theology were handed over to the church with no endorsement except "for study," they slowly have become the points of reference for varying new overtures and positions.

In 1980, the General Synod received three new overtures concerning homosexuality, one from the Classis of Wisconsin and two from the Classis of Schoharie. The second overture from Schoharie can serve as typical of all three. It urged the synod "to deny ordination into the ministry of the Reformed Church in America to practicing homosexuals and lesbians and to authorize the classes to demit from the ministry those who remain unrepentant of this sin." The advisory committee observed that since the Commission on Theology reports of 1978 and 1979 fully addressed "the belief that homosexual acts

---

[12] *MGS* 1979, 128–35.
[13] *MGS* 1979, 128.
[14] *MGS* 1979, 135.

are sinful" therefore, no additional word was necessary. The advisory committee further informed or reminded the General Synod that it "could not deny ordinations," since "only the classes can do that."[15]

Nine years later, acting on the recommendation of the 1989 Report of the Commission on Christian Action, the synod passed a resolution:

> To call upon members of the RCA to create a climate within the church whereby all persons will be truly accepted and treated as God's children, particularly women; persons with physical and mental disabilities; persons of various ages, language groups, and sexual orientation; and persons of other categories commonly discriminated against.[16]

The following year (1990), the General Synod received overtures from the Classis of Illiana and from the Regional Synod of Mid-America to amend this statement by deleting the words "and sexual orientation" from the 1989 text. The advisory committee recommended and the 1990 synod resolved:

> To call upon the members of the Reformed Church in America to create a climate within the church whereby all persons commonly discriminated against will be truly accepted and treated as human beings created in the image of God.[17]

The 1990 synod also received an overture from the Classis of Cascades urging the General Synod to adopt the 1978 Commission on Theology report "as the official position of the RCA on the subject [of homosexuality]." The advisory committee removed the phrase "official position" but recommended (and the synod voted) to " adopt as the position of the Reformed Church in .encouraging love and sensitivity toward such persons as fellow human beings."[18]

This is the first reference by any General Synod to the phrase "homosexual lifestyle." The advisory committee altered the language of the overture, omitting the word "official" and introducing the term "lifestyle." The advisory committee further recommended for synod "to instruct the Commission on Theology to conduct a new study on

---

[15] *MGS* 1980, 97, 284–85.
[16] *MGS* 1989, 81.
[17] *MGS* 1990, 460.
[18] *MGS* 1990, 461.

homosexuality and submit a report to the 1992 General Synod,"[19] as well as "to commend the papers [of the 1978 and 1979 Reports of the Commission on Theology] to RCA churches as pastoral advice until such time as a subsequent study by the Commission on Theology is approved by General Synod."[20] Synod passed both advisory committee recommendations and passed them on to churches as advice until such time as synod further refined its statements through further study.

The press of other studies previously assigned to the Commission on Theology resulted in a two-year delay of the new report, until 1994. The commission meanwhile engaged in a number of processes to assess the denomination's current concerns about homosexuality. In its 1994 study, the commission called for a new task force whose charge was a plan "to do justice to four basic concerns:

1. Concern for faithfulness to the word of God;
2. Concern for the unity of the church;
3. Concern for homosexual persons;
4. Concern for integrity of the church's moral witness in the culture."

In regard to the latter concern, while the commission suspected that "many Christians fear this issue cannot be resolved without one of these values being lost or compromised...the commission firmly believes, however, that this need not be the case."[21]

Early in their work, the task force and the commission determined that "they do not think the most helpful response at this moment is another position paper."[22] Therefore, they asked for two processes. The first assigns the commission/task force to:

1. Explore the issue;
2. Engage the denomination's membership in dialogue and discernment, seeking the Spirit when dealing with issues such as homosexuality;
3. Assist the membership in shaping attitudes and actions; and
4. Prepare a response based on insights gained from the process.[23]

The second process—intended for the denomination's membership—has five components:

---

[19] *MGS* 1990, 461.
[20] *MGS* 1990, 461.
[21] *MGS* 1994, 371.
[22] *MGS* 1994, 371.
[23] *MGS* 1994, 371–72.

1. An introduction to the diversity of opinions within the church regarding homosexuality;
2. A fresh design for biblical interpretation and its applicability;
3. A survey of the most recent learning from the social sciences;
4. An appraisal of ministry approaches past and present; and
5. A gathering of feedback from the denomination regarding the first four steps and the writing of a report aimed at furthering the ministry and mission of the church.[24]

When the advisory committee recommended the essential approval of the commission's report, the 1994 synod debate reverted to previous firmly held positions. Overnight, a small group of delegates developed—and in the morning presented—a substitute motion that called the church's membership "to a process of repentance, prayer, learning and growth in ministry" to be guided by the synod's statements of 1978, 1979, and 1990. The motion also called on the Commission on Theology to develop resources that would:

1. Assist congregations in understanding the import of the 1978 and 1979 reports;
2. Enable congregations honestly to face "the ways in which persons of homosexual orientation have wrongly suffered in our churches and in our society"; and
3. Provide a collection of models for ministry to homosexual persons.[25]

This substitute motion was adopted, and led to the publication of *Homosexuality: Seeking the Guidance of the Church*.[26]

For the next several years, the attention of the RCA regarding the issue of homosexuality was focused on our denomination's relationship with the United Church of Christ, especially as that related to our membership in the Formula of Agreement. During the 1998 General Synod, the general secretary of the Reformed Church in America addressed a concern in his report to the General Synod. The general secretary's concern was brought about by uproar following an action of the president of New Brunswick Theological Seminary, Dr. Norman J. Kansfield, and the seminary's board of trustees. Kansfield had appointed the Rev. Dr. Judith Hoch Wray, a New Testament scholar living in a

---

[24] *MGS* 1994, 372–73.
[25] *MGS* 1994, 375–76.
[26] *Homosexuality: Seeking the Guidance of the Church* (New York: Reformed Church in America, 1998).

committed relationship with another woman, to a one-year interim appointment as professor of New Testament Studies. Under pressure from denominational administrators and General Synod officers, the board of trustees rescinded the appointment, although several trustees indicated they were acting in violation of their consciences; the seminary board agreed to pay Dr. Wray the full value of the contract. Though Dr. Wray's contract was terminated prior to synod, the matter was slated as synod's first item of business.

In his report, the general secretary observed that "no issue has more capacity to confuse our focus, drain our energy, injure our fellowship, and divert our mission than this one. No current issue can so easily demoralize our meetings, paralyze our process, fuel our anxiety, and cripple our confidence as this one."[27] He therefore recommended that the synods of 1998, 1999, and 2000 would:

> refrain from deliberative debate and policy decisions relating to homosexuality...to instruct the General Synod Council, through the Congregational Services Unit, to enable congregations and classes to enter a process of intentional discernment concerning the pastoral challenges raised by the issue of homosexuality ...[28]

Dr. Kansfield, for his part, said,

> I assure you of my and New Brunswick's full future compliance with the part of the synod's recommendation which requests all commissions, agencies, assemblies, and institutions related to the General Synod to refrain from taking any action that would be in obvious contradiction of our stated positions...But, you know where my commitments lie. I ask you to count me among those who are committed carefully to listen to, and, as necessary, to speak on behalf of homosexual persons, most of whom will not feel free enough to participate in the church's important conversations.[29]

In 2004, six years after the above incident, Dr. Kansfield, who later said he was convinced that there was no constitutional hindrance to prevent this, agreed to preside at the marriage of his daughter, Ann, to Jennifer Aull on June 19, 2004, in the First Churches of Northampton,

---

[27] *MGS* 1998, 58.
[28] *MGS* 1998, 60.
[29] Norman J. Kansfield, manuscript of his report to the 1998 General Synod.

Massachusetts. Before this wedding, on June 9, 2004, President Kansfield notified the New Brunswick Seminary board of trustees of his intention to perform the wedding. The board neither warned him, nor asked for his resignation, nor fired him. Ten days before the wedding, the General Synod of 2004 voted "to affirm that marriage is properly defined as the union of one man and one woman, to the exclusion of all others,"[30] which was worded so as to target same-sex unions even though, if taken literally, it also forbids all forms of remarriage or second marriage. Dr. Kansfield was not present for the synod's vote.

By the beginning of 2005, four formal charges had been entered against Dr. Kansfield, three of which were deemed by the Investigative Committee to warrant trial. On January 28, 2005, the New Brunswick Board of Trustees voted to allow Dr. Kansfield's contract to expire June 30, 2005. The board later altered these terms, and his actual presidency ended with New Brunswick's 2005 commencement in May.

Because Dr. Kansfield held the office of General Synod Professor of Theology, his trial was to be held by the General Synod. Three charges were lodged against him:

1. The charge of "actions contrary to our faith and beliefs as affirmed by the Holy Scriptures and the decisions of the General Synod concerning the relationships of active homosexuality";
2. The charge that Dr. Kansfield contradicted his ordination declaration that stated: "I accept the Scriptures as the only rule of faith and life," as well as his affirmations stating "that I believe the Gospel of the Grace of God in Christ Jesus as revealed in the Holy Scriptures of the Old and New Testaments..."; that Dr. Kansfield contradicted his ordination promise to "walk in the Spirit of Christ, in love and fellowship with the church, seeking the things that make for unity, purity, and peace"; and
3. The charge that he failed to keep his promise to "submit myself to the counsel and admonition of the General Synod, always ready, with gentleness and reverence, to give account of my understanding of the Christian faith."

The trial proceeded, despite the fact that some RCA office bearers raised the issue that, in fact, Dr. Kansfield was no longer a General Synod professor, his employment having been terminated. Upon ending a presidency, the *Book of Church Order* calls for normal transfer of supervision to a classis for care and discipline.

---

[30] *MGS* 2004, 332.

Synod officers and parliamentarians dismissed this objection. The trial began as synod convened in the First Reformed Church in Schenectady, New York, on Thursday, June 16, 2005. The trial was the first item of business on the agenda that day, and continued through Friday, June 17, 2005. By the end of the afternoon session, synod voted Dr. Kansfield guilty of all three charges by very wide margins. That evening he was deposed from the Office of Professor of Theology and suspended from the Office of Minister of Word and Sacrament. A General Synod Pastoral Committee was appointed to care for Norman and Mary Kansfield. Ultimately, Dr. Kansfield's pastoral membership (under suspension) was transferred to the Classis of Rockland-Westchester. On October 20, 2009, following confession, repentance, and renewal of his vows, Dr. Kansfield was restored to the Office of Minister of Word and Sacrament.

Following this trial, the same synod that had convicted him also approved a plan for "an honest, intentional denomination-wide dialogue on homosexuality" as proposed in the report of the Commission on Christian Action. Three and one-half years were to be given to this process, for which the Rev. Dr. John Stapert served as facilitator. These dialogues continue in influence.

The General Synod of 2012 received overtures from several classes that urged the General Synod toward discipline of anyone holding a church office who acts to "encourage homosexual behavior" or preside at same-sex marriages. The advisory committee sought to combine these overtures into R-27, which evolved after discussion and parliamentary maneuvering, into a new motion called R-28.[31] It reads:

> While compassion, patience, and loving support should be shown to all those who struggle with same-sex desires, the General Synod reaffirms our official position that homosexual behavior is a sin according to the Holy Scriptures, therefore any person, congregation, or assembly which advocates homosexual behavior or provides leadership for a service of same-sex marriage or a similar celebration has committed a disciplinable offense; and further,
>
> the General Synod Council shall oversee the creation of an eight member committee made up of representatives appointed by each of the regional synods to pray and work together to present a way forward for our denomination given the disagreement in our

---

[31] *MGS* 2012, 145–50.

body relative to homosexuality. The purpose of the committee is not to revisit our stated position, but to operate with the understanding expressed earlier in this recommendation and issue a report with practical recommendations to the General Synod of 2013.[32]

The eight-member committee called for in R-28 was constituted in the summer of 2012 to take up its charge.

---

[32] *MGS* 2012, 149–50.

CHAPTER 15

What was the Reformation?[1]

The event called the Reformation of the 16th century has great importance for the Reformed Church in America. We remember and celebrate it as one of the foundations on which we stand, and we cherish the insights into the Christian faith that it has handed down to us.

What, then, *was* the Reformation?

Historians treat the Reformation as a broad, complex movement with many social, political, and economic aspects as well as religious ones, and they debate the question of when it can truly be said to have begun. But no one doubts that its famous public beginning point occurred in 1517, when the theologian Martin Luther published his so-called "95 Theses" against the selling of what were called "indulgences." And the insights that Luther expressed at that moment still serve, for us, as a key to understanding the Reformation.

At the heart of Luther's thinking was his conviction that God's saving forgiveness of sinful human beings was God's action, not ours—

---

1   *Minutes of General Synod* 2016 (New York: Reformed Church Press, 2016), 276–78. A video version of this paper, for use in small-group settings, is available at https://vimeo.com/179482645.

that it comes to us, that is, by God's "grace alone" (*sola gratia*), and is not contingent on anything that we do, or that the church does, but rather that we receive it passively, by "faith alone" (*sola fidei*), that is, by trusting God (this was his critique of "indulgences," whereby the Catholic Church itself had claimed a role in dispensing God's forgiveness).

Luther's central insight that our salvation comes only through God's grace, and not through our own works, was not a new insight. Luther himself had, of course, found it in the Scriptures, especially in the letters of Paul. And indeed this was an insight that had not been forgotten in the many centuries that separated Paul from Luther. The great church father Augustine of Hippo, most famously, had stated it very powerfully in the fifth century in his debates with the so-called "Pelagians," who had by contrast ascribed to humans an active role in their own salvation. Augustine's influence in this as in other respects remained strong within Catholic tradition, making its appearance in many contexts and with varied implications over time.

What was new, then, in Luther? What caused the sensation and upheaval in the years that followed in the wake of his publication of the Theses? The cause was not only his conviction—shared soon by others—of the principle of salvation by grace alone, received by faith, but the combination of this conviction with another increasingly shared conviction, one that in fact, in Luther's case, took a little while longer to clarify and had particular significance in his political and social context, where patterns of power in society were shifting. This was the conviction that the authoritative source of Christian truth was to be found in the "Scripture alone" (*sola scriptura*) as distinct from the church traditions that had interpreted it. In the case of indulgences and the theological understanding behind them, Luther was saying, the church had strayed from the truth that was in Scripture. This meant that the traditions of the church could in fact be wrong, and its authority thrown into question. It was this conclusion, as Luther and others would embrace it, that underlay the enormous changes in Christendom that were to follow, and to which we give the name Reformation.

So the Reformation stands as a fundamental and revolutionary *rethinking of the question of religious authority*. Those who came soon to be called "Protestants"—who included Luther and his immediate followers but also many others as well—elevated the Bible, as the Word of God, above all other presumed authorities, which they regarded as merely human. It is hard for us to grasp the significance of this rethinking. For it was not that the Catholic Church had ever rejected the authority of Scripture. On the contrary, the ancient Catholic tradition had established and conserved the "canon," that is, the list of books that constituted the Scripture. And the church, in continuity with that tradition, considered the Scripture, so constituted, as having been entrusted by Christ himself to his apostles and their successors—that is, to the church itself—as its guardian and interpreter. Thus the authority of the Scripture was of a piece with the authority of the church. And this conception of religious authority was part of the foundation of the very order of European society. What the Reformation did, in elevating Scripture above Church, was to undermine that foundation, and consequently that order: thus the upheaval.

The implications of this rethinking of religious authority were huge. For, once the authority of Scripture was elevated above that of the church, the obvious next question was: Who then decides what the Scripture means? Who interprets it? Indeed, a variety of groups and movements—"Protestants" of many stripes—emerged almost immediately, each claiming to interpret the Scripture definitively and differing not only from what they thought of now as the "Roman" Catholic Church (i.e., as one Christian tradition, indeed for them a false one), but also from each other, in matters small and large. The ostensible unity of Christendom was now destroyed. And even the Catholic Church, though it resolutely maintained its historic conception of itself in relation to Scripture, participated in this rethinking of religious authority, for, in reasserting its traditional doctrines at the Council of Trent (1545-63) and in a certain resurgence of its vitality in the years that followed, the Catholic Church implicitly acknowledged the new role that individual assent would have to play in the acceptance of these, within the new situation of a plurality of beliefs.

For us in the Reformed Church in America, the great legacy of the Reformation lies in this fundamental revision of the notion of religious authority that it brought about, and more particularly—to return to the concerns of Luther at its outset—in its guarantee of the great doctrine of salvation by grace alone, received by faith alone, and founded on Scripture alone. This doctrine has come down to us, not precisely through the legacy of Luther and his immediate followers the "Lutherans," who were concentrated in central Germany and Scandinavia, but rather through the so-called "Reformed" tradition, which began separately in the cities of Switzerland and spread to, among other places, the Netherlands, and with some distinctive traditions of its own—but which affirmed the same fundamental and scripturally based doctrine of salvation.

We remember and accept that doctrine of salvation as the Reformation's great legacy. But it is important to note, in closing, that we also acknowledge a tragedy of the Reformation, namely its violence. The plurality of religious groups that it engendered led to devastating "wars of religion," as the historians call them, which lasted through the middle of the 17th century. For though the Reformation inevitably raised the *question* of "who decides what the Scripture means?" it did not manage to find an answer that would allow adversaries to live together in peace. That is: in the time of the Reformation there was not yet (or there were only the barest glimmerings of) an idea of religious toleration. Such an idea was to take hold only later—in our case, especially in some developments in the Netherlands and in America in the centuries that followed, which we also remember and celebrate. But that is another story.

CHAPTER 16

Ecumenism in the RCA[1]

Four centuries ago, the Synod of Dort gathered in an attempt to extinguish the smoldering theological debate between Arminian Remonstrants and orthodox Calvinists, and in doing so, they welcomed ecumenical delegations from throughout Protestant Europe. At this pivotal moment in the development of both the theology and polity of the Dutch Reformed Church, representatives from the Church of England as well as churches in the Palatinate, Hesse, Switzerland, Geneva, Bremen, Emden, and France took part in the process of theological discernment.[2] Even in its nativity, the Dutch Reformed Church did not go it alone.

In the 400 years that have passed since the Synod of Dort, the Dutch Church and specifically its daughter church, the Reformed Church in America (RCA), has continued to wrestle with how to embrace calls for Christian unity, doctrinal purity, and denominational uniqueness. This paper provides an overview of the RCA's long history

---

[1] *Minutes of General Synod* 2018 (New York: Reformed Church Press, 2018), 284–89.
[2] Herman Harmelink III, *Ecumenism and the Reformed Church*, The Historical Series of the Reformed Church in America 1 (Grand Rapids, MI: Eerdmans, 1968), 7.

of ecumenical engagement and its efforts to balance an inclination toward ecumenical collaboration with a bent toward denominational independence.

Ecumenism during the Eighteenth and Nineteenth Centuries

The history of the RCA's ecumenical engagement begins in the eighteenth and nineteenth centuries. While the colonial churches often focused their energies on survival, especially after the British conquest of New Amsterdam in 1664, they also entertained calls to unify with other Reformed churches in the British colonies in North America. In fact, the Dutch churches nearly united with their Scottish Presbyterian and German Reformed counterparts in 1743 but were stymied by an inability to resolve the language differences between the three communions.[3]

At the same time, firebrand Theodorus Frelinghuysen exhibited an ecumenical disposition when he crossed denominational lines to partner with Presbyterian preachers like the revivalist Tennent family.[4] Despite dust-ups with his congregation and the Classis of Amsterdam, Frelinghuysen's flair eventually caught on with his Presbyterian neighbors and would go on to influence the most well-known evangelist of the Great Awakening, Calvinist Methodist George Whitefield.[5] While not solely responsible for this intercolonial and interdenominational religious awakening, Frelinghuysen's ecumenical ministry encouraged local collaboration and fostered a burst in evangelism.

After the American Revolution, the RCA successfully separated itself from the church in the Netherlands, yet even as it began to exercise its independence, the church entered into new ecumenical partnerships. During the period of the early republic, this was most evident in the church's missionary efforts. For example, in 1796, less than a decade after severing ties with the Reformed church in the Netherlands, the RCA lent its support to the New York Missionary Society.[6] This early

---

[3] Donald J. Bruggink and Kim Nathan Baker, *By Grace Alone: Stories of the Reformed Church in America*, The Historical Series of the Reformed Church in America 44 (Grand Rapids, MI: Eerdmans, 2013), 199.

[4] Thomas Kidd, *The Great Awakening: Roots of Evangelical Christianity in Colonial America* (New Haven: Yale University Press, 2007), 49.

[5] Kidd, *The Great* Awakening, 61–62; Harry S. Stout, *The Divine Dramatist: George Whitefield and the Rise of Modern Evangelicalism* (Grand Rapids, MI: Eerdmans, 1991), 93.

[6] Herman Harmelink III, "World Mission," in *Word and World: Reformed Theology in America*, ed. James W. Van Hoeven, The Historical Series of the Reformed Church in America 16 (Grand Rapids, MI: Eerdmans. 1986), 77.

missionary society focused on ministry to the Native Americans, and John Livingston—the father of the RCA—even served the organization as one of its earliest officers.

The New York Missionary Society marked the beginning of the RCA's engagement with ecumenical missionary efforts. In 1810, the RCA partnered with the American Board of Commissioners for Foreign Missions (ABCFM), which operated as an ecumenical missionary organization during the first half of the nineteenth century. Influential and pioneering Dutch Reformed missionary John Scudder stands out as just one example of some of the prominent RCA missionaries who received their initial support from the ABCFM. Despite its engagement with the ABCFM, in 1832, the RCA founded its own Board of Foreign Missions, which initially worked in conjunction with the ABCFM before ending the partnership in 1857.[7]

Regardless of the RCA's disassociation with the ABCFM, seven years later the denomination was heralded for its "pioneering leadership in missionary ecumenism."[8] This was largely due to the efforts of a host of RCA missionaries who worked in tandem with other Protestant missionaries throughout the globe, particularly in China, India, and the Middle East.[9]

The ecumenical mission in Amoy, China, offers an illuminating example of the ecumenical nature of the RCA's robust missionary apparatus. Throughout the 1850s, a fruitful partnership existed between missionaries from the RCA and English Presbyterian missionaries in Amoy. An organic union grew between these two missionary groups, and together they founded a small network of Chinese churches. The biggest conflict that arose for the mission in its early years came about due to pressures from the General Synod to tamp down the ecumenical nature of the mission and force sole affiliation with the RCA. A heated scuffle lasted from 1857 to 1863. The missionaries resisted, but the General Synod was insistent. Eventually, after threatening to resign, the missionaries won the day, and the General Synod adopted a more cooperative posture toward ecumenical missions.[10]

While the hullabaloo about the Amoy mission presents a striking example of the tensions that came along with ecumenical mission work, its ecumenical character was not unique. In 1872, the RCA's

---

[7] Harmelink, "World Mission," 79–80.
[8] Quoted in Harmelink, "World Mission," 87.
[9] Harmelink, "World Mission," 89.
[10] Harmelink, "World Mission," 82, 84–85.

Japanese mission followed Amoy's example and united with the English Presbyterians.[11] Similarly, nineteenth-century missionary work in India, led by the Scudder family, and in the Middle East, led by men like Samuel Zwemer, nurtured ecumenical partnerships.[12] In the twentieth century, the RCA's missionary work in Africa would exhibit the same ecumenical impulses.

Throughout the nineteenth century and into the twentieth century, the RCA's most prominent and successful ecumenical endeavors centered on its commitment to missionary activity. Through both institutional affiliations with groups like the ABCFM and also local, ecumenical collaboration between individuals, ecumenism in the RCA became associated with spreading the gospel and an extensive missionary network.

Twentieth-Century Institutional Affiliations

Throughout the twentieth century, the RCA explored membership in a number of larger ecumenical bodies, and these conversations incited a bevy of debate and disagreement within the denomination. The earliest—and least controversial—of these broader church affiliations brought together various Reformed churches throughout the world. Founded as the Reformed Churches throughout the World holding a Presbyterian System in 1875, the group now known as the World Communion of Reformed Churches (WCRC) functioned as a space for theological discussion and fellowship.[13] The RCA joined this communion as a founding member and has continued to engage in this forum for global Reformed theological discussion.[14]

The RCA's membership in other national and global associations proved to be far more contentious than its participation in the WCRC. For instance, in 1908, the RCA became a founding member of the Federal Council of Churches, which would become the National Council of Churches (NCC) in 1950.[15] Similarly, the RCA was also a charter member of the World Council of Churches, which was established in 1948 in the aftermath of World War II.[16] Both groups brought together diverse communions not only for theological discussion but also for

---

[11] Harmelink, "World Mission," 85.
[12] Harmelink, *Ecumenism*, 25.
[13] Bruggink and Baker, *By Grace Alone*, 198.
[14] Bruggink and Baker, *By Grace Alone*, 200.
[15] Harmelink, *Ecumenism*, 56; Bruggink and Baker, *By Grace Alone*, 203.
[16] Bruggink and Baker, *By Grace Alone*, 204.

cooperative action through relief efforts, publications, and other joint endeavors.

Despite initial enthusiasm about these ecumenical bodies, opposition to the RCA's membership in both of these bodies arose shortly after the denomination joined them. The first objections arose in 1930.[17] Since then, fears about the formation of a unified church or significant doctrinal differences have flared intermittently and led to attempts to withdraw the RCA from both bodies. In fact, the General Synod of 1969 saw the denomination nearly withdraw from the NCC, and similar debates took place throughout the 1980s.[18] Nevertheless, the RCA remains a member of both of these larger organizations.

While the RCA embraced the ecumenical efforts of the NCC and WCC, it stalwartly resisted joining the Consultation on Church Union (COCU), which arose in the mid-twentieth century in order to explore the possibility of union between a diverse group of denominations, ranging from Presbyterians to Methodists and Congregationalists. The RCA never became an official member of this organization but did maintain observer status. It ultimately rejected participation due to suspicions about the organization's aims and a firm commitment to the uniqueness of the Dutch Reformed tradition.[19]

At the close of the twentieth century, rather than pursue organic union between denominations, the RCA, along with many other denominations, worked to recognize full communion between distinct denominations.[20] In particular, at the behest of the Evangelical Lutheran Church in America (ELCA), the RCA explored the possibility of greater cooperation between Reformed and Lutheran churches in the United States. These efforts led to the Formula of Agreement, which was signed by members of the RCA, Presbyterian Church (USA), and the United Church of Christ (UCC) with the ELCA in 1998.[21] This agreement accomplished two primary goals. First, it rescinded four centuries of anathemas that had existed between Reformed and

---

[17] Lynn Japinga, *Loyalty and Loss: The Reformed Church in America, 1945–1994*, The Historical Series of the Reformed Church in America 77 (Grand Rapids, MI: Eerdmans, 2013), 34–35.

[18] Lynn Japinga, "On Second Thought: A Hesitant History of Ecumenism," in *Concord Makes Strength: Essays in Reformed Ecumenism*, ed. John W. Coakley, The Historical Series of the Reformed Church in America 41 (Grand Rapids: Eerdmans, 2002), 24; Japinga, *Loyalty and Loss*, 217.

[19] Japinga, *Loyalty and Loss*, 270–72.

[20] Herman Harmelink III, personal communication, December 19, 2017.

[21] Bruggink and Baker, *By Grace Alone* 205.

Lutheran communions, dating back to the Reformation era. Second, it acknowledged mutual recognition of sacraments and ministers between each of these four denominations. This has led to the opportunity for Lutheran and Reformed ministers to serve in one another's churches, a development that was paralleled with the unification of Lutheran and Reformed churches in the Netherlands into The Protestant Church of the Netherlands.[22]

Much like other ecumenical efforts throughout the twentieth century, the Formula of Agreement provoked disagreement within the RCA. This opposition initially focused on the UCC's open stance toward LGBTQ clergy and same-sex marriage—a position that both the PC(USA) and ELCA would also eventually take.[23] Yet, the Formula of Agreement provided for "mutual admonition" between denominations, which has led to many of those who oppose the position of the other members of the Formula of Agreement to exercise this clause to admonish views that conflict with the RCA's own position on these particular social issues.

Twentieth-Century Unification Efforts

The RCA exhibited considerable handwringing about its membership in larger ecumenical bodies throughout the twentieth century, but even more heated disagreement arose regarding unification with other Reformed denominations. The RCA was not immune from the ecumenical fervor that led to a spate of mergers during the twentieth century, but ultimately, despite numerous appeals to join other like-minded traditions, the RCA chose to remain independent.

In 1945, the RCA explored a union with the United Presbyterian Church in North America (UPC), a small Presbyterian denomination located in Ohio and Pennsylvania. These efforts failed.[24] Many members of the RCA, particularly in the Midwestern classes, feared the loss of denominational identity and the familial feeling they associated with the RCA. Others suggested that just because two traditions had much in common did not mean that they needed to merge with one another. Christian unity could exist spiritually while structurally remaining separate. In the end, the General Synod voted in favor of the union, but only 19 classes approved of it, far short of the 34 required by the commission overseeing the union.[25]

---

[22] Harmelink, personal communication.
[23] Harmelink, personal communication.
[24] Japinga, *Loyalty and Loss*, 47.
[25] Japinga, *Loyalty and Loss*, 53.

Ecumenism was still in the air in the early 1960s. The General Synod of 1962 received eighteen overtures about union—eight for the Presbyterian Church in the United States (PCUS), eight for the UPC, one for the UCC, and one for the Christian Reformed Church (CRC). The RCA chose to explore a proposed merger with the PCUS—the southern Presbyterian Church.[26]

When the General Synod voted to move ahead with a committee to explore the union in 1965, opposition was already on the rise.[27] Objectors feared a loss of denominational uniqueness and the dilution of Reformed doctrine. What is more, in 1966, PCUS joined the COCU, a perennial lightning rod for controversy in the RCA.[28] Despite this move by the PCUS, the General Synod of 1968 approved the merger. Nevertheless, the classes rejected it, with all of the classes east of Detroit voting in favor and all those west of it voting against, for a final vote of 23 for union and 22 against, well shy of the two-thirds approval required.[29]

Since the first efforts to unite the church with other Reformed traditions during the colonial era, the RCA has entertained 12 attempts to unite with another denomination.[30] All have failed. Yet, in each case, serious talks have taken place.[31] This willingness to explore the possibility of union exhibits the RCA's underlying ecumenical commitment. Throughout these efforts, there have been both cultural and theological reasons for resisting mergers that reflect a fear of losing the distinctly Dutch Reformed theological tradition, most evident in our creeds and confessions. There was also a fear that these mergers might lead to a slippery slope of mergers first with larger Presbyterian bodies and eventually even larger bodies like the COCU.[32]

A Special Relationship to the Christian Reformed Church

While many proposed mergers between the RCA and other Reformed traditions took place throughout the twentieth century, one denomination was conspicuously absent but must be a part of any

---

[26] Japinga, "On Second Thought," 19.
[27] Japinga, "On Second Thought," 21.
[28] Japinga, *Loyalty and Loss*, 109, 113.
[29] Japinga, "On Second Thought," 25; Japinga, *Loyalty and Loss*, 138.
[30] Herman Harmelink III, "Ecumenism and the Reformed Church Revisited," in *Concord Makes Strength: Essays in Reformed Ecumenism*, ed. John W. Coakley (Grand Rapids, MI: Eerdmans, 2002), 3.
[31] Bruggink and Baker, *By Grace Alone*, 199.
[32] Japinga, "On Second Thought," 14, 17.

discussion of the RCA's relationship with other denominations: the Christian Reformed Church (CRC).

Prior to the two major secessions that led to the establishment of the CRC, the RCA was not a stranger to internal division. Some of the most rancorous debates dated back to colonial disputes between Coetus and Conferentie, which began in the 1730s.[33] Unlike those early divisions, which eventually healed, the nineteenth-century divisions between the RCA and the CRC remain; however, in many ways the CRC has become the RCA's closest partner.

The two primary moments of secession took place in 1857 and 1882. The first division reflected tensions in the Midwestern immigrant community about the Classis of Holland's affiliation with the RCA in 1850.[34] The division that occurred in 1882 also originated in the Midwest; however, it focused on disagreements between the immigrants and the American church about the role of freemasons within the church.[35] For decades, these disagreements had flared at General Synod. The latter secession strained the relationship with the mother church of many of the immigrants, the Christelijke Gereformeerde Kerk in Nederland, which meant many new immigrants chose to join the CRC rather than the RCA.[36]

Over the past half century, the RCA's relationship to the CRC has warmed significantly. At the request of the CRC, more open dialogues began in the late 1960s.[37] The CRC harbored anxieties about the RCA's ecumenical memberships in the NCC and WCC and a perceived lack of enforcing doctrinal purity by the RCA. These talks in the 1960s eventually waned and ultimately ended without any result.[38]

More recently, a renewed partnership has arisen between these our two denominations. This is most evident in joint publications, shared missions, and simultaneous annual meetings.[39] In 1999, Maple Avenue Ministries in Holland, Michigan, became the first congregation to hold

---

[33] Gerald F. De Jong, *The Dutch Reformed Church in the American Colonies*, The Historical Series of the Reformed Church in America 5 (Grand Rapids, MI: Eerdmans, 1978), 190–191.

[34] Elton J. Bruins and Robert P. Swierenga, *Family Quarrels in the Dutch Reformed Churches in the 19th Century: The Pillar Church Sesquicentennial Lectures*, The Historical Series of the Reformed Church in America 32 (Grand Rapids, MI: Eerdmans, 1999), 87–88.

[35] Bruins and Swierenga, *Family Quarrels*, 108, 116–17.

[36] Bruins and Swierenga, *Familiy Quarrels*, 131.

[37] Harmelink, personal communication.

[38] Harmelink, personal communication.

[39] Harmelink, personal communication.

dual membership in both the CRC and RCA.[40] More recently, the dual denominational membership of Pillar Church in Holland, Michigan, marked a significant symbol of ecumenical partnership and healing between these traditions due to its role as Albertus Van Raalte's church and as the site of the particularly acrimonious secession of 1882.[41] The RCA has continued to grow closer to the CRC into the twenty-first century, signaling a promising future of ecumenical engagement.

Local Ecumenism in the Past Half Century

The history of the RCA's involvement with ecumenical movements tends to focus on denominational affiliations, initiatives, and efforts; however, ecumenism in the RCA also includes pastors like Frelinghuysen and Livingston and the host of missionaries who served throughout the globe. These individuals suggest that an essential element to the history of ecumenism in the RCA is the role of local churches engaging in ecumenical partnerships in order to serve their communities.

A brief historical case study illuminates how a local church, even in a small town in the Midwest, exhibits the RCA's ecumenical commitments. Over the past half century, Sanborn First Reformed Church (FRC) in Sanborn, Iowa—a town of 1,300 residents with eight churches—has embraced ecumenism as a means of fulfilling their call to ministry. For more than three decades, the church has hosted the only vacation Bible school that 289 attracts children from all of the other churches in town. FRC participates in communitywide luncheons during Lent that draw members from both the town's Protestant and Catholic churches and takes a leadership role in the coordination of community worship services. What is more, for over a decade, it jointly hired a youth pastor with a United Methodist Church in the next community in order to offer robust youth programming to its children. In this rural community, for the past 50 years, FRC has provided a model for ecumenical leadership.

Sanborn FRC is not unique in its classis, synod, or the RCA. A history of collaborative ecumenical engagement exists in churches ranging from Highland Park, New Jersey, to Paramount, California, to Grand Rapids, Michigan. From volunteers from New York churches serving during Billy Graham's crusades in 1957 to ecumenical children's

---

[40] "Maple Avenue Ministries," Christian Reformed Church, accessed February 14, 2018, www.crcna.org/churches/5147.
[41] Harmelink, personal communication.

programs in rural Iowa, RCA churches have a history of adapting the tradition's ecumenism to their needs and context. A shared commitment to the Gospel and a desire to serve local communities remind us that the history of ecumenism in the RCA is not solely one of failed mergers and spats about association memberships. It is a story of a people striving to fulfill their call to mission.

CHAPTER 17

Anabaptist and Reformed Relations: A Historical Overview[1]

In the preface to its 1793 Constitution, the Reformed Protestant Dutch Church in North America recognized that the harsh language within our confessions could cause other Christians to take offense. It states:

> In publishing the Articles of Faith, the Church determined to abide by the words adopted in the Synod of Dordrecht ... in consequence of which, the terms alluded to could not be avoided. But she openly and candidly declares that she by no means thereby intended to refer to any denomination of Christians at present known, and would be grieved at giving offence, or unnecessarily hurting the feelings of any person.[2]

This disclaimer refers to the strong denunciations of some other Christian groups within our confessions, specifically the Anabaptists in

---

[1] *Minutes of General Synod* (hereafter *MGS*) 2019 (New York: Reformed Church Ppress, 2019), 272–76.
[2] *The Constitution of the Reformed Dutch Church in the United States of America* (New York: William Durell, 1793), vii.

the Belgic Confession. Articles 18, 34, and 36 of the Belgic Confession condemn Anabaptists by name, rejecting and, at times, mischaracterizing their views of the incarnation, baptism, and the church's relationship to civil governments.

Today, 226 years after the publication of this original disclaimer and 458 years after the Belgic Confession was penned, the Reformed tradition's understanding of these key theological tenets still differs from the Anabaptists; however, the use of terms including "heresy," "condemn," and "reject" no longer reflect the spirit of ecumenical partnership that now exists between our traditions. Because our confessions are "historical and faithful witnesses" to our faith, we cannot simply revise our confessions, omitting difficult passages. Instead, the church must appreciate what they signified at the time and wrestle with how we might reconcile ourselves to groups that are condemned within them today. This paper attempts to address these themes, offering a brief overview of relations between Reformed and Anabaptist Christians in both sixteenth-century and modern-day contexts. Key to this study are the following questions: Who are the Anabaptists? What is their legacy? Why is reconciliation important? How might Reformed Christians relate to them today?

Who are the Anabaptists?

Anabaptist—which means "rebaptizer"—is a pejorative label that was given to Anabaptists by their disapproving Catholic and Protestant neighbors during the Reformation era. As historians have noted, there are several problems with this title.[3] For one, Anabaptists do not believe in re-baptizing, but in adult baptism; for them, infant baptism is not a legitimate baptism since it is not explicitly commanded in Scripture. Second, the title suggests that baptism was the most important issue for the Anabaptists. In fact, baptism was an incidental doctrine. What was most important for the Anabaptist movement was their doctrine of the church (ecclesiology) and accompanying theology of discipleship, both of which focused on what it meant to be a community that lived in active obedience to the Scriptures.[4] Third, the name seems to suggest that theirs was a unified movement. In actuality, several Anabaptist movements emerged almost simultaneously and independently in Switzerland, different parts of Germany, Austria, Moravia, and the

---

[3] Denis R. Janz, *A Reformation Reader* (Minneapolis: Fortress Press, 2008), 183.
[4] Willem Balke, *Calvin and the Anabaptist Radicals* (Grand Rapids, MI: Eerdmans, 1981), 11.

Netherlands.⁵ While there were significant differences of theology and practice among the movements that developed in these locations, some core beliefs can be identified among the Anabaptist groups. These include pacifism, separation of church and government, voluntary church membership, separation from worldly corruption, and church discipline.

The pursuit of peace is one of the central tenets of the Anabaptist tradition. This manifests most obviously through Anabaptists' rejection of violence in any form and the high premium they place on peace.⁶ Anabaptists adopted the Reformation principle of *sola scriptura*, a mantra meaning Christians should base their beliefs solely on the words contained in Scripture. Unlike other Protestant traditions springing up during this era, Anabaptists interpreted Scripture to place a clear prohibition on violence and to elevate the pursuit of peace. The Anabaptist tradition, therefore, traditionally avoids war and violence and even in the face of persecution tends to choose non-violent resistance. This pursuit of peace extends to the Anabaptist belief in seeking harmony and unity with other Christians and within their own communion as well. Peaceful coexistence with other Christians became a key belief of the Anabaptist tradition, particularly in the centuries following its establishment in the sixteenth century. This hallmark of the tradition remains with the Anabaptists today, offering an example of how to pursue peace in even the most divisive times.

Anabaptists also have a distinctive interpretation of the relationship between the church and state, being pioneers in arguing for a strict separation between the church and the state. They made this argument on the basis of their belief that state meddling in the church represents a significant threat to the purity of the church.⁷ Conversely, they feared that when the church got involved in politics, it would inevitably lead to external influences on the life of the church. Any engagement between the church and the state had the potential to taint the witness of the church. They took this possibility extremely seriously. For centuries, Anabaptists held this position, often placing themselves in peril due to persecution from governments controlled by Reformed, Lutheran, Anglican, and Catholic traditions. Even today,

---

[5] James R. Payton Jr., *Getting the Reformation Wrong: Correcting Some Misunderstandings* (Downers Grove: IVP Academic, 2010), 163.
[6] Alister McGrath, *Historical Theology: An Introduction to the History of Christian Thought* (Oxford: Wiley-Blackwell, 2013), 129.
[7] McGrath, *Historical Theology*, 129.

most Anabaptists strenuously guard against any entanglement with politics in an effort to protect the integrity of their faith. In the name of preserving the purity of the gospel, most Anabaptists do not run for elected office or attend political rallies.

What Is the History of Reformed–Anabaptist Engagement?

A common misconception concerning the religious history of the sixteenth century is that there was a single European reformation, which began with Martin Luther and continued through his successors, branching off into other evangelical (later called Protestant) churches, beginning with the reforms of Huldrych Zwingli. Today, scholars of the Early Modern period largely agree that there was not one but multiple reformations, some of which began before Luther, such as Wycliffe's reforms in England, and at least two others that began in the sixteenth century but are not considered part of the Protestant Reformation. These are the Catholic and Radical reformations. The magisterial (Protestant) reformers, including John Calvin, Luther, and Zwingli, understood their own theological situation in opposition to both of these other parties. On the one hand, they set out to reform the Roman Catholic Church to more faithfully reflect the apostolic church that Christ founded. On the other hand, they sought to distance themselves from the Anabaptists of their time, who they perceived as "radical" in their sacramental theology, ecclesiology, eschatology, and practices. In 1539, Calvin protested in his letter to Cardinal Sadoleto, "Two parties militate against us; they are as different as they possibly can be. Because what does the party of the Pope have in common with the Anabaptists?" Despite the diverse beliefs of the Reformation movements that emerged during this era, Catholics and nearly all Protestant groups agreed in their condemnation of Anabaptist theology and viewed it as a threat to the delicate social order in a season of tremendous instability.

The rejection of the Anabaptists extended far beyond denunciations within Reformed confessions. Rather, the violent persecution brought upon the Anabaptists in the sixteenth century was often at the behest of Reformed Christians, particularly those living in Zurich under the direction of Zwingli. Among the many Anabaptists who were persecuted was Felix Manz, a former student of Zwingli, who was sentenced to death by drowning in the Limmat River on the orders of the Zurich city council. Making a mockery of his convictions on adult baptism, the city council ordered Manz's hands tied behind his back and executed him by plunging him into the icy river. A Hutterite chronicle from 1542 details several other inhumane acts against Anabaptists, including the burning of Wolfgang Ullmann in Waltzra, Switzerland, and the beheading of ten men and drowning of their wives in Swabia, Germany. The chronicle recounts that the persecution of Anabaptists in the area finally

> ... reached the point that over twenty men, widows, pregnant wives, and maidens were cast miserably into dark towers, sentenced never again to see either sun or moon as long as they lived, to end their days on bread and water, and thus in the dark towers to remains [sic.] together, the living and the dead, until none remained alive ... There was issued a stern mandate at the instigation of Zwingli that if any more people in the canton of Zurich should be rebaptized, they should immediately, without further trial, hearing, or sentence, be cast into the water and drowned.[8]

These types of persecutions continued until the end of the eighteenth century.[9]

Movement toward Reformed–Anabaptist Cooperation

In the last century, great strides have been made toward healing the divisions that were created in the sixteenth century between the Reformed and Catholic churches. For example, the RCA has participated in a national dialogue between Reformed churches and the Roman Catholic Church for the last five decades. Through this dialogue, participating churches continue to move toward reconciliation as they now formally recognize each other's baptisms and acknowledge each other's churches as those in which the body of Christ is truly present. But while significant attention has been given to repairing the rift between Catholics and Reformed Christians, there has been no formal process in place for seeking reconciliation with our Anabaptist brothers and sisters.

Today, three major groups of Anabaptists trace their lineage to their sixteenth-century predecessors: the Mennonites, the Amish, and

---

[8] George Hunston Williams, *Spiritual and Anabaptist Writers* (Philadelphia: Westminster Press, 1957), 45.

[9] Peter Dettwiler, "Mennonites and Reformed—A Process of Reconciliation," in *Steps to Reconciliation: Reformed and Anabaptist Churches in Dialogue*, ed. Michael Baumann (Zurich: Theologischer Verlag Zürich, 2007), 20. John Calvin also wrote much about his opposition to Anabaptism in general and Menno Simons (the Dutch leader of the Mennonites) in particular.

the Hutterites. Related groups emerged in later centuries that bear a similar theology and practice, such as the Bruderhof communities and the Schwarzenau Brethren (or German Baptist Brethren). While some Anabaptist views have become more "mainstream"—it has been suggested that a diffuse Neo-Anabaptist movement is emerging in the U.S., represented by theologians and church leaders such as Stanley Hauerwas, Ron Sider, and Brian McLaren, whose core beliefs include pacifism and social justice—traditional Anabaptists (Mennonites, Amish, and the Hutterites) are still marginalized in American Christianity. Much of this is due to a lack of understanding and familiarity with Anabaptist beliefs and practices. But such intolerance also demonstrates the tenacious hold that the Reformation perspective still has on the Reformed imagination. For centuries, our churches have defined their identity in their opposition to other churches. Like the reformers, Reformed Christians today continue to identify themselves in negative disassociation from "radical" groups like the Anabaptists.

While there has been a noticeable absence of attempts to formally pursue reconciliation in the U.S., important initiatives have been taken at the international level to heal historic wounds. In 1983, the World Alliance of Reformed Churches hosted a Day of Encounter, celebrating a decade-long dialogue with the Baptist World Alliance. Alongside Baptist and Reformed delegates, Mennonites were invited as well. The service ended in a common celebration of the Lord's Supper. The hopes for reconciliation that were sparked at the conference were fanned into a more robust flame through an international dialogue between the World Alliance of Reformed Churches and the Mennonite World Conference. These moments of communion remind us of the bonds we already share with Anabaptists through ecumenical bodies such as Christian Churches Together, the National Council of Churches, and the World Communion of Reformed Churches.

In 2004, the Church of Zurich also took a powerful step toward rapprochement, hosting a conference titled "The Reformation and the Anabaptists—Steps to Reconciliation." Mennonite and Reformed Christians worshiped together in a service of reconciliation that included the confession of sins against Anabaptists and a petition for healing and unity. But the major contribution of the occasion was the presentation of a tablet that commemorated the execution of Felix Manz and other Anabaptists and was dedicated on the site of Manz's death.

During the 2004 event, Reformed Christians in Zurich declared that, "It is time to accept the history of the Anabaptist movement as part of our own, to learn from the Anabaptist tradition, and to strengthen our mutual testimony through dialogue."[10] The clarion call of the Zurich Christians is one that goes out to the RCA to consider as well: It is time to underscore our common heritage in Christ, to learn from each other, and to strengthen our witness through our pursuit of unity. As stated at the beginning of this paper, there were indeed many reformations during the sixteenth century. That said, the many sixteenth-century reforms shared a common goal—to more faithfully reflect Christ's intentions for the church. According to 1 Corinthians 12, the church that Christ calls us to and into which we are baptized—as infants or as adults—is one body in Christ. There is "no division in the body, but that the members may have the same care for one another. If one member suffers, all suffer together; if one member is honored, all rejoice together." The acknowledgment that the RCA is only one part of the larger body of Christ, which also contains the Anabaptists, frees us to learn from our Anabaptist brothers and sisters, to hear and honor their stories of persecution, to listen to their views on pacifism, to glean from their robust theology of discipleship, and to be shaped by their rich sense of community. They teach us compelling lessons about the pursuit of peace, wariness about comingling between the church and politics, and the virtues of a robust theology of discipleship.

What Might Future Reconciliation Look Like?

What might reconciliation between Anabaptist and Reformed Christians look like in our own context, initiated by our own communion, and at this time? This history reveals a need to lament that we have not lived into Christ's prayer for unity, to acknowledge the fracture between our two communions, and to repent of our role in forming this division. If we begin with repentance, might we ask Anabaptists what reconciliation should look like, being responsive to the aggrieved party, allowing Anabaptists to inform us about how we might begin the process of reconciliation?

---

[10] Peter Dettwiler, "The Anabaptists Inheritance in Ecumenical Dialogue—A Reformed Perspective," in *Steps to Reconciliation*, 40.

www.ingramcontent.com/pod-product-compliance
Lightning Source LLC
Chambersburg PA
CBHW070755100426
42742CB00012B/2138